D1129073

Applying Family Therapy

THE PERGAMON TEXTBOOK
INSPECTION COPY SERVICE

An inspection copy of any book published in the Pergamon International Library will gladly be sent to academic staff without obligation for their consideration for course adoption or recommendation. Copies may be retained for a period of 60 days from receipt and returned if not suitable. When a particular title is adopted or recommended for adoption for class use and the recommendation results in a sale of 12 or more copies, the inspection copy may be retained with our compliments. The Publishers will be pleased to receive suggestions for revised editions and new titles to be published in this important international Library.

SOCIAL WORK SERIES

Editor: Jean P. Nursten

Other Titles in the Series

Applying Family Therapy

A PRACTICAL GUIDE FOR SOCIAL WORKERS

by

Helen C. Masson and Patrick O'Byrne
Huddersfield Polytechnic, UK

PERGAMON PRESS
OXFORD · NEW YORK · TORONTO · SYDNEY · PARIS · FRANKFURT

U.K.	Pergamon Press Ltd., Headington Hill Hall, Oxford OX3 0BW, England
U.S.A.	Pergamon Press Inc., Maxwell House, Fairview Park, Elmsford, New York 10523, U.S.A.
CANADA	Pergamon Press Canada Ltd., Suite 104, 150 Consumers Rd., Willowdale, Ontario M2J 1P9, Canada
AUSTRALIA	Pergamon Press (Aust.) Pty. Ltd., P. O. Box 544, Potts Point, N.S.W. 2011, Australia
FRANCE	Pergamon Press SARL, 24 rue des Ecoles, 75240 Paris, Cedex 05, France
FEDERAL REPUBLIC OF GERMANY	Pergamon Press GmbH, Hammerweg 6, D-6242 Kronberg-Taunus, Federal Republic of Germany

First edition 1984
Reprinted 1985

Library of Congress Cataloging in Publication Data

Masson, Helen C.
Applying family therapy.
(Social work series)
Includes bibliographical references.
1. Family social work—Great Britain.
2. Family social work—Great Britain—Case studies.
3. Family social work—Study and teaching—Great Britain.
4. Family psychotherapy—Great Britain—Case studies.
I. O'Byrne, Patrick. II. Title. III. Series.
[DNLM: 1. Family therapy. 2. Social work. WM 430.5.F2 M419a]
HV700. G7M34   1984   362.8'253'0941   83–19293

British Library Cataloguing in Publication Data

Masson, Helen C.
Applying family therapy.—(Social work series)
1. Family psychotherapy
I. Title   II. O'Byrne, Patrick   III. Series
616.89'156   RC488.5

ISBN 0–08–030186–X (Hardcover)
ISBN 0–08–030187–8 (Flexicover)

Printed in Great Britain by Redwood Burn Limited, Trowbridge

Preface

In this book we are aiming to provide a clear, straightforward account which will enable the reader to apply the method of family therapy to practical situations. In particular we are offering advice and suggestions about how to get started with family therapy, our experience indicating that this often presents problems for practitioners.

We believe that this book will be of help to student social workers and to social workers who are already qualified but who have little knowledge or experience of the method. (Most social workers trained before the 1970s will have had little or no teaching in family therapy.) In a multidisciplinary context we think this book will also be of interest and use to teachers, psychologists (clinical and educational), doctors, psychiatrists, marriage guidance counsellors, other counsellors employed, for instance, in the armed forces, and clergy, particularly those involved very heavily in pastoral work.

Although the book is written in a British context we believe that our approach is readily applicable to work with families in other countries. For the benefit of readers abroad who are not familiar with the British social work context, however, we offer here a simple description of social work in this country. Social workers are usually employed either in public welfare agencies (e.g. Local Authority Social Services Departments [which include hospital settings] and Education Social Work Departments, or Probation Departments) or in voluntary, charitably-based agencies (e.g. Dr. Barnardo's, National Society for the Prevention of Cruelty to Children, Family Service Units). Social workers in such agencies cover a range of work with and on behalf of families and they may be involved in situations where court duties or orders are in force (e.g. supervision orders, care orders, social enquiry reports of various kinds). In these situations families do not pay for the services of the agencies though there are also some private, fee-paying based agencies which offer help to individuals and families. In order to obtain the basic professional social work qualification students undertake a course leading to the Certificate of Qualification in Social Work. There are approximately 50 non-graduate and 60 graduate C.Q.S.W. courses in this country. Most are two-year courses. Beyond basic professional qualification there are numerous employer and nationally run post-qualification courses available for social workers to update and expand their knowledge and expertise.

v

We have received much support and encouragement in the preparation of this book. In particular we would like to thank Judith Milner and Chris Gwenlan who took time out to read an early draft and who offered us much useful criticism and suggestions for improvements. Responsibility, however, for the final copy rests with us. We would also like to thank our families for their patience and encouragement whilst we worked to complete this project.

HELEN C. MASSON AND PATRICK O'BYRNE

Contents

Introduction

This book arises out of our longstanding and developing interest in family therapy, an interest which is expressed in two ways: in practice and teaching. Currently we are both employed as lecturers on a course leading to the Certificate of Qualification in Social Work (C.Q.S.W.) but our backgrounds are in a Children's and later Social Services departments (HM) and in the Probation Service (PO'B). Having discovered our mutual interest in family therapy and having realised that our styles and theoretical orientations to the work were similar and complementary, we decided to join forces as a co-therapy pair and to offer our services to families in trouble. To this end we successfully applied to be Probation volunteers with a local department and then "advertised" for work.

We had intended to collect together a number of case studies before considering publication at all but various factors have made us rush, perhaps the reader will feel precipitously, into print! Most importantly, over the last four or so years we have shared our particular approach to work with families with several groups—practitioners employed in three social work agencies (via short courses and on-going seminars), teaching colleagues and students on the C.Q.S.W. course to which we are linked. From all these quarters we have received sufficient positive feedback and interest to feel that perhaps a larger audience might find some of our theoretical and practical preferences helpful in their own practice. Our ideas do seem to be especially helpful as regards *getting started* with family work and our experience to date indicates that this seems to be an area of real difficulty for many people. There are probably a number of reasons for this—apprehension about meeting with a group, anxiety about the possibility of making mistakes, the off-putting jargon in some of the literature and the mystery that is sometimes associated with the whole approach. So, our aim in this book is to present the way we tackle work with families in a straightforward, reasonably simple and readable form so that practitioners will be encouraged to actually take the plunge and try out some family therapy ideas in practice. The other major consideration was that although our co-therapy work progresses slowly (our teaching and other commitments mean we can only work with one family at a time and referrals are not always immediately forthcoming) we record in great detail work with each family and we think one family's case especially can be usefully employed as an illustrative base on which to build the rest of the book. We have, of course, obtained the written consent of the family to

ix

use their case in this way and we have omitted or altered any details that might identify them. Thus, obviously, we are not claiming to offer a fully researched, objectively evaluated account of work with families (though we recognise such studies are badly-needed). Rather we are attempting to explain our theoretical approach and in particular *how we apply* theoretical ideas and techniques to work with families, using, in this instance, one case study to highlight what we outline.

We have taken to heart Phyllida Parsloe's comment that some social workers, when asked to evaluate their training and practice, reported that, in relation to family therapy, their C.Q.S.W. training "had been no help. It had been based on the American literature of family therapy grounded in work with middle class, fee-paying clients in private agencies, which bore little relation to the setting or the clients of a local authority."[1] We hope that, with other "home-grown" literature[2,3,4] this book makes at least a small contribution to practice within British social work settings. We certainly think that the Green family, whose circumstances and difficulties we describe, is fairly typical of the sorts of family situations which confront social workers in both voluntary and statutory settings but we think it is important to make clear here ways in which our work diverges from much current social work practice. In our approach we place great emphasis on the need, for instance, for thorough planning, recording and evaluation of work and on the need for consultative and supervisory provision. It seems that such emphases are at odds with recent descriptions of at least some social work practice.[5,6] Moreover, in discussion with practitioners, it has become clear that reorganisation to allow for specialisation within teams and the development of the expectation that work can be shared very productively may be important underpinnings if family therapy is to be effectively applied to work with some families. We do not, however, apologise for our ideas. Not only do we think that planning family sessions in detail can be enormously helpful in overcoming one's fears about getting started, but also we think that the above are aspects or principles of practice which are essential whatever social work method is being attempted, if work is to be effective and seen to be effective. For instance, detailed planning and recording of work saves a great deal of time in the long run because one's overall purposes, goals and means of achieving them are that much clearer. On a hopeful note, from our own experience we are aware of much innovative and thoughtful work being undertaken even within the confines of a traditionally organised social-work setting.

We do not present our work with the Green family as an example of a flawless piece of practice. On the contrary we are aware that we did not understand all that we should have done, we know we made mistakes in the course of our sessions with the family. While we are rather anxious about "exposing" our errors in this book, we do not, however, think that errors in themselves are necessarily to be regretted. We go along with the view of Selvini Palazzoli and her colleagues in Italy that errors are essential to learning in family therapy. They argue that therapeutic interventions are no more than a learning process acquired through trial and error. They equate trying to understand and help families with a rat learning to negotiate its way through a maze though, of course, they point out that families are much more complicated than mazes because they are constantly changing in response to new circumstances and developing relationships and feelings. Selvini Palazzoli and Co. argue that one only makes an error if one fails to consider the information gleaned from one's excursions![7] In other words what is important is to learn from the mistakes one makes. Certainly our experience accords with this view and as we shall show when describing our work with the Green family we not only use the feedback from our mistakes to deepen our understanding of family dynamics but also we use the information gained directly in subsequent sessions with the family.

Finally then let us explain the layout of this book. In Part I we outline the theory and techniques which are influencing our work with families. We have found, when presenting our work to colleagues in various agencies, that it is not enough to simply describe what we do. We are always asked to identify and explain our use of theory. Our audiences are usually well aware that the term "family therapy" covers a whole range of theoretical orientations and practical ideas for family work[8] and so it is important that we start by making our "allegiances" clear in order to avoid misunderstanding and muddle. In addition, of course, many social workers, trained on an essentially psychodynamic model, have real difficulty in understanding our systems based, "here and now" approach without being offered some initial theoretical foundation. Chapter 1 then sets the scene by outlining our theoretical understanding of families and of how problems arise in families. In Chapter 2 we define our aims as family therapists and we offer some suggestions for when family therapy may be the method of choice when attempting to modify some problematic family situations. We describe our preferred theoretical approach to family therapy, a task-centred approach, and hence the techniques and strategies we employ, in Chapter 3 and in Chapter 4 we discuss the potential strengths and weaknesses of co-therapy in work with families.

Apart from occasional references to other cases, Part II is given over to a description of the work we undertook with the Green family. As we have already indicated we are describing the full process of work with one family in order to illustrate our approach, not to provide evidence of its validity. We have, of course, adopted the same theoretical and practical approach to work with other familes to good effect, which makes us more convinced of its value, but we would not want the reader to jump to the conclusion that we are seeking to infer too much from the case. Our hope is that by describing the case-work in full, from beginning to end, "warts" and all, the reader will find our description more real, convincing and helpful in terms of putting flesh on the theoretical bones outlined in the first part of the book. Perhaps it is important to make another point clear in relation to the Green family case presentation. We have said earlier that we are enthusiastic about planning and evaluating work but obviously we do not envisage that other workers would need to record their efforts with families in the same detail that we do in Part II of the book. We process recorded every interview for our own interest and professional development and for teaching and discussion purposes. It would be quite unnecessary and indeed impractical for full-time practitioners to record in such detail. Briefly outlining Part II of the book, then, Chapter 5 contains details of the referral we received about the family and the agreements we made with the referral agent. Chapters 6 to 11 include discussions of various aspects of work with families, using the six sessions we had with the family to illustrate these aspects—beginning work and engaging with families, exploring a family's difficulties, working with parental and sibling sub-systems, evaluating, consolidating and terminating work. In each of these chapters the actual interviews we had with the whole family or parts of it will be described in considerable detail on the left hand side of the pages, with comments and notes on the process recorded on the right. When appropriate we will use charts, diagrams and pictures of sculpts to illustrate our analysis. The last chapter, Chapter 12, will include some summarising and evaluative thoughts on our work.

We hope that the reader will enjoy this book and that after digesting our ideas and techniques he or she will *try some of them out in practice*. We will especially welcome criticisms and suggestions flowing from such applications.

References

1. *Social Service Teams: The Practitioner's View,* DHSS, P. 341 (1978).
2. *Journal of Family Therapy,* published by Academic Press, London.
3. Walrond Skinner, S., *Family Therapy: The Treatment of Natural Systems,* RKP (1976).
4. Walrond Skinner, S., (Ed.), *Family and Marital Family Psychotherapy,* RKP (1979).
5. *Social Service Teams: The Practitioner's View,* DHSS, Chapters V, VII, VIII (1978).
6. Goldberg, E. Matilda and Warburton, R. William, *Ends and means in social work,* NISS Lib. No. 35, GAU (1979).
7. Selvini Palazzoli, M. S., Boscolo, L., Cecchin, G. and Prata, G., *Paradox and Counterparadox: A New Model in the Therapy of the Family in Schizophrenic transaction,* Jason Aronson Ltd., London (1978—English translation).
8. See Barker, P., *Basic Family Therapy,* Granada, London, for a useful summary (1981).

Theorising about Families and Family Therapy

CHAPTER 1

Families and Family Problems

In this chapter and in the rest of Part I of this book we will briefly outline the kinds of theoretical ideas which help us to make sense of a family's dynamics and which give us ideas about how to intervene in problematic family situations. As will become apparent we find ourselves to be very much in sympathy with the work of people like Haley, Minuchin, Watzlawick, Weakland, Cade and, more recently, Selvini Palazzoli.

But first what do we mean by the word family? When we try to define this social unit we find ourselves thinking in terms of role structures, blood ties, marriage ties, affectional ties and intensity of interaction between people and the fact of common residence. There are, therefore, many ways in which a family can be defined but we prefer the definitions of families which emphasise the meaning families have for their members. For instance Pollak (1965) suggests that a "family exists when people related to one another by blood or the sharing of a home consider themselves resources for one another on a more comprehensive basis and at a higher degree of intensity than they consider other people."[1] Thus relatives not living in a family's household may be of great significance within a family's system (e.g. grandparents, ex-spouses) as may be non-relatives either living in the household (e.g. lodgers) or outside it (e.g. non-related "Aunts" and "Uncles"). The significance of these people may lie in the positive consequences they have on family functioning, as Pollak's definition suggests, but of course it is just as possible that their significance is related to negative aspects in family dynamics. What *is* important is to chart the extent (or perimeter) of a family's system. Otherwise work may be thwarted because important people in the system are not actively involved in treatment when they ought to be, or at the least, their impact on the family's dynamics is inadequately understood. (See Skynner's article (1971) on engaging with the operative emotional system for a fuller discussion of this.)[2] When we accept a referral about a family one of the first things we do is to draw a family tree or genogram based on the information we have been given (as we will demonstrate in Chapter 5 when we describe how we first heard about the Green family). This helps us to be aware of the possible "significant others" who are not actually part of the family household or part of the immediate nuclear family group.

Families as systems, organisations and as changing social units

We have already used the word "system" in our opening remarks to this chapter and certainly when we discuss and analyse a family's unique life style and problems we draw on General Systems Theory ideas. Of course, a systems approach to social work is not new—see, for instance, Pincus and Minahan (1973).[3]

Walrond-Skinner (1979)[4] argues, in fact, that all family therapists must inevitably have a basic systems orientation to families given that they are all interested in the "interpersonal processes and behaviours occurring between the members of a natural psychosocial system, the family, and between the family system and its environment". She describes General Systems Theory (GST) very fully elsewhere (1976)[5] but simplifying matters considerably families can be seen as being made up of various sub-systems (marital, parental, parent-child and sibling sub-systems) which are, in turn, made up of individual personality systems. The whole family itself can be seen as a system, having points of exchange with systems outside of itself such as the extended family, neighbourhood systems, educational, religious, economic and political systems. Thus, imagining a nuclear family made up of two adults and two children, a diagram of the family system within its environment might look something like this:

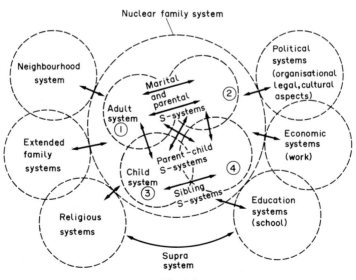

Fig. 1.1

Around individuals, between the various sub-systems and between any one family and its environment (or supra-system) are boundaries, but boundaries which should allow for contacts and exchanges to take place so that the usual ebb and flow of life and adaptation to changing circumstances can occur. Various writers have described family systems with too loose or too rigid boundaries either within the family system itself or between the family system and its supra-system. Skynner (1974)[6], for instance, believes that if boundaries are too open or permeable "the organism is flooded and over-whelmed with sense impressions, invaded by the psychological contents of other individuals with whom the person comes into contact, with a resulting fluctuation and lack of clarity of identity sense or even psychosis. By contrast if psychological boundaries are too impermeable we get stability at the expense of extreme defensiveness, rigidity and so impaired growth, development and creativity."

As a simplified example of excessively open intra-family boundaries one can imagine a family where people within the family do not allow each other psychological and physical space or privacy. People may think they know how others are thinking and feeling and may not bother to check these assumptions out through listening and discussion. They may actually *tell* others how they are (or should be) thinking and feeling. Eventually people may not know where they end and others begin as it were; they become unsure of their own wishes, responses and identities. Over time, communication patterns within such families are rendered extremely confusing and distorted. As an example of a family whose boundary with its supra-system is too open, imagine the situation where, when one makes home visits, the household is usually full of people (not always the same people either), some relatives, some friends, who get involved in "personal" aspects of the life of the family in an intrusive, unhelpful way and who sit in on every discussion unless a determined effort is made to persuade them to leave. They enter the house without knocking, sit around as if they are in their own home and are only too eager to offer their "two-penny worth" on the basis of scant knowledge or understanding of the family's difficulties.

When boundaries are too rigid one may find that a family is cut off from outside involvements in the neighbourhood or community; closed to influences from outside of itself. Rigid boundaries between members within a family would be evidenced by people's inabilities to empathise with each other, to see things from differing perspectives. Family members might be unable to adapt to changing circumstances, being preoccupied with preserving themselves intact and unchanged in defensive ways. Sharing of feelings, ideas and wants would probably be threatening.

Schizophrenagenic families, Skynner suggests, are characterised by excessively permeable boundaries between the individuals in the family but at the same time too rigid and impermeable boundaries between the family and the outside world so that therapeutic inputs are blocked. Jordan (1976)[7] would describe such families, which bind family members together "in a sometimes confusing and mystifying way, to the exclusion of the outside world" as integrative but argues that they represent "only one extreme in a continuum, at the opposite end of which are those families in which members seek to escape from all involvement with each other by fleeing from the family into the outside world".[8] Such families he calls centrifugal families. Jordan discusses how ordinary families exhibit both integrative and centrifugal tendencies and in his book he discusses how social factors external to the nuclear family (supra-system) will effect the balance of these forces within the family. (The impact of the supra-system generally will be discussed in the next paragraph.) Minuchin (1974),[9] who calls too rigid boundaries "disengaged" and too diffuse boundaries "enmeshed" argues, like Jordan, that normal families may exhibit both aspects in different sub-systems, or at different times without problems, but he too suggests that problems are likely to develop if family systems are chronically highly enmeshed because they do not allow enough autonomy for individuals and sub-systems, or if they are highly disengaged because there is a consequent lack of support for stressed individuals or sub-systems. We will return to these sorts of ideas shortly when discussing the organisational and structural aspects of families.

A crucial aspect of a systems orientation to the family is the notion that the functioning and features of the family system and any of its sub-systems will be affected by what is happening in those sub-systems and in the supra-system, (because of the relatively open boundaries existing between the system parts which allow for transactions to take place). This means, of course, that changes occurring in any part of the total system will have reverberations or effects elsewhere. To take a simple example: if a major breadwinner in a family, often the male adult in this Society, has to give up work (through illness or redundancy perhaps) this is most probably going to affect his self-image, have an impact on his functioning in his marital and parental roles and hence alter somewhat the family as a whole. In addition, of course, the responses of others in the family to him in this situation will be modified and so one can imagine a series of reverberating impacts. Two treatment implications arise out of this. Firstly it is, therefore, tremendously important to fully assess *how* and *where* a problem is being created and maintained because this will indicate where the focus for one's problem-solving efforts should be—whether it be with a system smaller or larger than the family system itself. Some writers suggest that not enough attention is paid to the impact of the supra-system on families. Kingston (1979),[10] for instance, argues that sometimes problems in family and marital relationships may be wrongly attributed to individual or family pathology when, in fact, understanding has to be sought within the wider economic, political and socio-cultural aspects of the supra-system. However, whether one can then affect the necessary changes in those aspects of the supra-system (and by what means) is another whole area for (often) hot debate which we do not propose to stray into. In this book we are focusing on family problems which seem to be maintained *within* that family system which thus becomes the focus for interventions.

The second point to be made is that if, as we have just noted, change in one part of a total system does have ripple effects throughout the system then one does not need to work with whole systems all of the time in order to modify their functioning. So, in relation to helping a family system in difficulties, family therapists may decide that work with one or more family members on an individual basis, or work with two or more people in a sub-system relationship or work with combinations of individual, sub-group and whole family interviews may be most productive. Where one would pitch one's efforts would be based on judgements about, for instance, what goals had been agreed with the family, the best "points of leverage", the availability, practically and motivationally, of family members, and assessments about which parts of the system needed strengthening and clarifying. As will be described in later chapters, in our work with the Green family, we chose to meet with the whole family, with Mrs. Green and Mr. Williams together and with the children as a group in order to affect change.

Arising out of G.S.T. are two other concepts in particular which have important implications for work with families. First of all there is the concept of homeostasis. Systems work to maintain themselves in a steady state. Applying this concept to families, this means that families establish, consciously and unconsciously, ways of dealing with everyday living which become habitual, unquestioned and often valued. These "ways of dealing" are more usually called interactional patterns, sequences of behaviour or transactions and we will discuss these more fully when we look at the second G.S.T. concept of non-summativity. Suffice it to say at this stage that these transactions may either promote the well-being of the family system and its family members (functional) or, over time at least, they may lead to the creation and maintenance of problems in families (dysfunctional). But whether functional or not it is not easy to modify such patterns of interaction because of the tendency of systems to maintain themselves as they are. There is, in other words, an inbuilt resistance to change which family therapists have to be aware of if they are going to be successful in their work with families. This resistance may be achieved through a variety of means. One way involves disqualification. In dysfunctional families members have a tendency to disqualify each other frequently in both what is said and done. Attempts are made to "prove" people wrong in their beliefs and actions or what they say and do is evaluated as worthless, stupid, or not worthy even of attention. Similar means may be used to counter a worker's efforts to modify a family's difficulties. The family may resist change by seeking to demonstrate, for instance, that the worker is on the "wrong tack" in his perceptions or that he is unsuccessful in his attempts to improve things. Family therapists, therefore, may have to help families acknowledge and feel sure that change is necessary, possible and not unacceptably threatening. In Chapter 3 we will suggest ways in which this may be achieved.

The second concept from G.S.T., which we have already identified, is that of non-summativity or the notion that the whole is more than the sum of its parts. In order to understand and help a family it is not enough to study the individuals within that family, nor the various sub-systems they inhabit. It is not enough to study these parts of a family to see how they "tick", with a view to adding up their various characteristics and behaviours in order to arrive at an appreciation of the family as a whole. Instead one must observe the interactions *between* people within systems, one must understand the typical ways in which they relate to each other and how, therefore, they modify each other. Walrond-Skinner (1976)[11] likens this process to understanding the game of chess. She comments that one cannot understand that game by just looking at the pieces, "one would need to examine the game as a whole, and to take note of how the movement of one piece affects the position and meaning of every other piece on the board. (Similarly) . . . the nature of the transactional processes between family members transcends the activity of individual family members themselves when viewed in isolation".

What then, in more detail, are these transactional processes and patterns? They are, of course, the contacts and exchanges between wholes and parts of systems; they are the means by which families maintain their "steady state". They include things like the usual verbal and nonverbal patterns of communication through which people relate to each other and the ways in which roles and functions are allocated to and expressed by family members. They also include the tacit or clearly stated values, rules and assumptions on the basis of which family life is managed, the rituals, traditions, myths and secrets which develop over time and the typical ways in which families react to and cope with both normal changes in circumstances and abnormally stressful events.

One can become aware of such transactional processes and patterns through asking oneself questions about how people are interacting with each other. Here are examples of some of the questions that could be posed:

A. Are people able to be honest with each other about factual matters and about positive and negative feelings? Can people admit problems to each other and be open about what they want from each other?
B. How skilled are people at listening to each other?
C. How do people negotiate about things and decide on issues? Can they compromise?
D. How are family responsibilities shared out?

E. Do people demonstrate positive feelings for each other verbally and nonverbally? Does the family have any fun together?
F. Are individual differences and growth needs allowed for? But are appropriate limits set too (evidenced in words like "No", "not now" and "that's enough")?
G. Are family interactions characterised by excessive amounts of any of the following: evasions/denials; double messages; answering or speaking for others; giving orders; placating; blaming; sarcastic comments; inappropriate jokes; interruptions; put downs; bribes/threats; defiance and rule breaking?
H. Is there evidence of collusions, scapegoating, hidden agendas (relating to an individual's unspoken needs, wishes or emotional conflicts), assumption making, secrets, myths or taboos (deliberately unshared information, deliberately kept family fiction, forbidden subjects), power struggles, lack of boundaries or too rigid boundaries?[12]

These transactions seem to develop a semi-autonomous life of their own to which people within the system become habituated. Consequently system "inmates" may find it difficult to modify their ways of interacting with each other, from within the system. For instance, people may assume that the "rules" by which their family manages its affairs possess some kind of "god-given" quality; that, therefore, the rules cannot be changed and that, therefore, they cannot help things being as they are. In this discussion we are referring to those kinds of rules (functional or dysfunctional) which only become apparent in a family's transactional patterns, patterns which result in people commenting on the lines of "this usually happens as a rule" or, for instance, "we keep avoiding each other but we should be enjoying things together". Such rules characterise and regularise interactions. Family therapists joining the system, but coming from outside of it, may be able to help them to query their assumptions and may be able to redefine things or make suggestions so that family members are enabled to alter those aspects of their transactions which, though familiar and routinised, are now creating difficulties for them.

In order to more fully understand the nature of these transactional processes and the sorts of problems which often develop we have turned to the work of people such as Minuchin and Haley. Minuchin, for instance, in his book *Families and Family Therapy* (1974)[13] talks about a family's structure, "the invisible set of functional demands that organises the ways in which family members interact." Families, he says, carry out their functions through their sub-systems, each sub-system having rather different functions. In a nuclear family, for instance, the spouse or marital sub-system, which Minuchin sees as a refuge from the multiple demands of life, must develop interactional patterns in which each spouse supports the other's functioning in many areas, practically and emotionally. In addition this sub-system must establish clear boundaries between itself, its own parental system, the children and grandparent sub-systems. The parental sub-system's main task is to develop ways of tackling the socialisation of the children, ways which are flexible enough to accommodate the changing needs of growing children. How to protect, control, guide and assist one's children to independence have all to be worked out by this sub-system. The sibling sub-system is the place where children can begin to learn about peer relationships, where they can learn how to negotiate, bargain, share and cooperate with each other. In these respects it is important that the sibling sub-system is allowed some space, some privacy by the other sub-systems so that children can develop their own interests, can experiment and can learn from the mistakes they will inevitably make.

Haley (1976)[14] describes similar sorts of ideas in terms of family hierarchies of power and status based on things like generation, age and sex. Both he and Minuchin then go on to discuss how the transactional patterns or sequences of behaviour as Haley calls them, which regulate family members' behaviour and through which the functional demands of the family are met, are maintained not only by the idiosyncratic expectations of family members and family traditions, but also by universal rules and metarules, rules about rules. A metarule is a principle for interpreting rules. For instance "conformity to social norms" may be the metarule in force when domestic chores are allocated in a family. Similarly relationships have to be worked out in terms of their degrees of complementarity and symmetry. A complementary relationship is one in which unequals complement each other—there is, in power terms, a higher and lower participant, e.g. pupil-teacher; a symmetrical relationship is one that exists between equals, e.g. two friends. In marriage the relationship may be a mixture of both types—the partners may agree to give each other areas of control, e.g. the husband may be happy to allow his wife to make all the decisions about culinary matters and household decorations, she in return may wish him to be the dominant partner in their sexual relationship, taking the initiative on most occasions. These are two examples of complementarity. In the area of finance and budgeting, however, they may operate in symmetry, both working out problems together as equal partners. Of course where metarules are not agreed or accepted a power struggle is likely to ensue. In relationships between parents and young children there is usually the metarule in operation that parents should have greater authority than children in a family, i.e. they should enjoy complementary relationships. There are also metarules about how giving and taking people should be. The rule of mutual devotion operates where each is sensitive to the other's needs and tenderly cares for the other without seeking reward. This level of altruism, especially if it is expected permanently, is unrealistic. While such devotion operates on occasions a more realistic style is that of positive reciprocity, i.e. fair shares, *quid pro quo* agreements. People do things for each other in the expectation that they will get something back in return. (By the time we enter families as therapists we often find they have deteriorated into patterns of interactions characterised by negative reciprocity—family members are stuck in habits of giving tit for tat, injury for insult.)

Given these structural and organisational aspects of families what can go wrong? Let us offer some examples. Minuchin, who describes things in terms of boundaries between sub-systems being broached, suggests problems may arise, for instance, if grandparents interfere with the management of the family's functioning in ways that undermine the marital and particularly parental sub-systems. Haley describes such problems in terms of chronic, secret coalitions which cut across family hierarchies and which are evident in repetitive sequences of behaviour. For instance, as an example of a three generational conflict, he describes a typical sequence of behaviour existing between a grandmother and a mother and a child in a one parent family:

"1. Grandmother takes care of the grandchild while protesting that mother is irresponsible and does not take care of the child properly. In this way grandmother is siding with the child against the mother in a coalition across generation lines.
2. Mother withdraws, letting grandmother care for the child.
3. The child misbehaves or expresses symptomatic behaviour.
4. Grandmother protests that she should not have to take care of the child and discipline him. She has raised her children and mother should take care of her own child.
5. Mother begins to take care of her own child.
6. Grandmother protests that mother does not know how to take care of the child properly and is being irresponsible. She takes over the care of the grandchild to save the child from mother.
7. Mother withdraws, letting grandmother care for the child.
8. The child misbehaves or expresses symptomatic behaviour.

At a certain point, grandmother protests that mother should take care of her own child and the cycle continues, for ever and ever. Included in the cycle, of course, is sufficient misbehaviour or distress by the child to provoke the adults to continue the cycle."[15]

(It would be so easy for a social worker to see grandmother as a useful resource which needs to be supported and encouraged, without realising the pattern of interaction and its circular consequences.)

A classic example of a two generational conflict, which Minuchin describes, is the sort of family situation where the mother has taken on responsibility for everyone and everything in the family and where father has become a very peripheral figure. The mother will often present as over-whelmed and martyred and may complain that her husband does not support her with the care and control of the children. However, observing family interactions indicates that if father does ever intervene (at mother's insistence often) his efforts may be undermined by subsequent maternal activities and/or he will be accused of not understanding things properly or of handling situations badly. He will, therefore, withdraw, so allowing the sequence of behaviour to repeat itself endlessly. We shall return to this theme of circular causality in a later chapter.

Another typical problem arises if the parental sub-system is intruded by a child, if the child tries to become parent to his or her siblings, "*if* the delegation of authority is not explicit or if the parents abdicate, leaving the child to become the main source of guidance, control and decisions."[16] Apart from the fact that this state of affairs will probably place too great a strain on a child's capacities and will therefore interfere with his developmental needs, as Haley comments, the metarule about parents having greater authority than children in families has been violated and in all likelihood some of the loudest protests will come from the child's siblings, who expect to have a symmetrical relationship with him or her and who resent his or her apparent elevation to the parental ranks. In fact, as already indicated, the parental child's position is often very tenuous indeed because he or she may possess very little actual power, it not being officially delegated by the parents.

Families which are being reformed as a result of divorce, temporary or permanent separations or widowhood may get into all sorts of difficulties if the new sub-system boundaries are not clearly established to everyone's satisfaction, if the transactional patterns which define the boundaries are not drawn up with reference to the sorts or rules already described. In this context the special problems relating to step-parenting are, we think, worthy of a mention. Society itself is not sure about how step-parents should function within families and so the chances of difficulties arising whilst, for instance, natural and step-parents work out issues of complementarity and symmetry in their parental functioning *vis à vis* their own and each other's children (who themselves are negotiating new sub-system relationships) are very high indeed. Maddox (1976)[17] and Robinson (1980)[18] offer some very useful information and advice on how to help families with step-parents. For instance, Maddox suggests that as a first step in work a new "rule" should be established that step relatives should not expect or be expected to immediately love or even like each other. "How should step relatives behave? They should be freed from the idea they must love each other and behave as parent and child. All that should be demanded on both sides is politeness. If love grows, well and good."[19] (Later on in this chapter we will elaborate on this kind of intervention, when we discuss what we mean by first and second order changes.) As regards temporary separations, many Probation officers will have had experience of helping an ex-prisoner to re-estab-lish himself within his family's structure and functioning. Ireland and Dawes in their article (1975)[20] describe a family where the husband had served a number of prison sentences and had been absent through many of the important years of the development of his children. His wife had had to assume responsibility for family affairs and difficulties had arisen when he had tried to re-negotiate a place for himself within the marital and parental sub-systems.

And then, as a final example, there are the families exhibiting chronic boundary problems such as those where, as Minuchin[21] puts it, "one sub-system uses the same nonmember to diffuse sub-system conflicts." This is seen most commonly when parents use a child to take the focus off their own conflicts. Such situations are described by Vogel and Bell (1960)[22] in their article entitled "The emotionally disturbed child as a family scapegoat". In our own experience we have been working recently with a family where the teenage daughter was presented as the one with problems. Indeed her behaviour at school and at home was difficult and demanding and she had been placed on a supervision order as a result of offences of theft and an assault on a girl. However, it quickly became apparent that the girl's behaviour was very much related to how she was being handled by those around her and so far as the home situation was concerned it was the fact that her parents could not agree on matters of discipline and more or less overtly sabotaged each other's efforts to manage family affairs that "allowed" their daughter to take control in destructive ways. When we then looked at her parents' relationship with increased interest the "cracks" quickly became very apparent in their marital as well as their parental sub-system function-ing. Interestingly, thinking back to our comments on the tendency of families to resist change, when we touched on these aspects in our explorat-ory first session with the family this must have been seen as a great threat by the mother in particular. She used various people (including her mother and the Probation Officer involved) to try and put us off visiting a second time. However, with tact and "concerned persistence" we stayed engaged with the family and our work subsequently focused openly and productively on the relationship between the girl's parents. She was no longer reported to be any particular problem to the family. Indeed we think she felt a bit "miffed" at being out of the centre of the stage. Of course this is one of the dangers when working with a family that has been scapegoating one of its members. There are attractions of a sort in being in such a key position.

Having now discussed families as systems and as organisations with structures and rules we now need to introduce a third perspective on families, families as changing entities. This may surprise the reader as we've already indicated that families have homeostatic tendencies, that is they attempt to maintain a steady state. Certainly there *are* strong forces in families towards system maintenance but in addition families have to be able to adjust to the changes occurring over time which are related to the growth and developing needs of its individual members. This is where the concept of the Family Life Developmental Cycle is particularly relevant, a concept which develops Minuchin's ideas about sub-systems functions. Walker (1977)[23] defines the concept thus: "The life cycle defines sequential stages occurring throughout a typical family career, basing the stages on the major developmental tasks being faced by the family". There have been a number of different classificatory schemas of the normal family life cycle, a famous one being the eight stage cycle described by Duvall.[24]

LIFE CYCLE STAGE

I	Married couples (without children)
II	Childbearing families (oldest child from birth to 30 months)
III	Families with pre-school children (oldest child from $2\frac{1}{2}$–6 years)
IV	Families with school children (oldest child from 6–13 years)
V	Families with teenagers (oldest child from 13–20 years)
VI	Families as launching centres (first child gone to the last)
VII	Middle aged parents (empty nest—grandparenthood)
VIII	Ageing family members (retirement, death of one and then both spouses)

Each of these stages has clearly defined characteristics, each requires the performance of certain developmental tasks and each successive stage demands appropriate adjustments from members of the family group. For instance let us look at a six stage family cycle suggested by Carter and McGoldrick (1980)[25] in which they identify what they reckon are the tasks being faced by family members at each stage:

STAGES OF THE FAMILY LIFE CYCLE

Stage	Emotional process of transition: Key Principles	Second order changes in family status required to proceed developmentally
1. Between families: the unattached young adult	Accepting parent-offspring separation	(a) differentiation of self in relation to family of origin (b) development of intimate peer relationships (c) establishment of self in work
2. Joining of families: marriage	Commitment to new system	(a) formation of marital system (b) realignment of relationships with extended families to include spouse

3. The family with young children	Accepting new members into the system	(a) adjusting marital system to make room for children (b) taking on parenting roles (c) realignment of relationships with extended family to include parenting and grandparenting roles
4. The family with adolescents	Increasing flexibility of family boundaries to include children's independence	(a) shifting of parent-child relationships to permit adolescents to move in and out of the system (b) refocus on midlife marital and career issues (c) beginning shift towards concern for older generation
5. Launching children and moving on	Accepting a multitude of exits and entries into the family system	(a) renegotiation of marital system as a dyad (b) development of adult-adult relationships between grown children and their parents (c) realignment of relationships to include in-laws and grand-children (d) dealing with disabilities and death of parents (grandparents)
6. The family in later life	Accepting the shifting of generational roles	(a) Maintaining own and/or couple functioning in face of physical decline: exploration of new familial and social role options (b) support for a more central role for middle generation (c) making room in the system for the wisdom and experience of the elderly: supporting older generation without over-funtioning for them (d) dealing with loss of spouse, siblings peers and preparation for own death. Life review and integration

As Scherz (1970)[26] points out, the shift to each new developmental stage, with its different tasks, can be described as a "transitional stress point" and indeed this would be in accord with our view earlier expressed that families tend to maintain a steady state and resist change. "Each developmental phase and stress point within a family", Scherz continues, "requires new identifications, alliances, role transitions and family rules" which create stress and which thus "contain the potential for crises out of which can come constructive resolution, stultifying regression or chronic difficulties."[27] Haley (1973)[28] would agree that family stress is highest at the transition points from one stage to the next and Minuchin (1974)[29] states "with this orientation (of the family life developmental cycle) many more families who enter therapy would be seen as average families in transitional situations, suffering the pains of accommodating to new circumstances." This is a helpful notion, we think, because it emphasises the normality of many family difficulties and indicates that stress and strain are normal features of all families. Thus, for instance, at stage 5 of Carter and McGoldrick's family cycle quite normal difficulties may be encountered when the middle-aged adults are faced with renegotiating their marital relationship which may have become rather submerged under their parental functioning in the previous 15 or so years. If these difficulties are mishandled in some way, then problems are likely to develop. For instance, if the parents have "lived only for the children" and fear discovering a "non-relationship" with each other, they may try to maintain their children as children, preventing them from "launching" themselves and not allowing them to interact with themselves on a more adult like basis. And yet, at the same time, the parents may complain that their children are not growing up and taking responsibility for themselves and that therefore their own lives are being made a misery.

Of course, some families will have, potentially at least, a rather easier passage than others. Some families will have to cope with the relatively common but more stressful phases associated with separation, divorce and remarriage, for instance, and some families will have their capacity to meet the demands of each successive developmental stage reduced through factors within the family (illness, accident, death, birth of a handicapped child) or outside of it (poverty, economic depressions, the effect of social policies, wars).

How families often develop problems

We have now looked at three frameworks which help us to analyse family life (families as systems, organisations and as changing social units). In the course of this description we have given examples of *what* sorts of problems may arise. Now, in the final part of this chapter, we want to look in a little more detail at *how* such problems often develop. Here we will be drawing in particular on the ideas of Watzlawick *et al.* (1974)[30] and Weakland *et al.* (1974).[31] In keeping with a systems perspective they view problems that people seek help with as problems of interaction, and building on family life developmental cycle ideas they remark that such problems are primarily "an outcome of everyday difficulties, usually involving adaptations to some life change, that have been mishandled by the parties involved. When ordinary life difficulties are handled badly unresolved problems tend increasingly to involve other life activities and relationships in impasses or crises and symptom formation results."[32] Thus they make a useful distinction between ordinary, normal *difficulties* and *problems* which are the result of chronic mishandling of the very same difficulties.

So how might problems develop out of normal difficulties? Watzlawick *et al* reckon that there are two main ways that this might happen. First of all people may not recognise that they have an ordinary or worse difficulty facing them that needs some response; they deny that a potential problem exists at all. Parents may pretend that their children are not growing up and do not need to be allowed greater independence, husbands and wives may insist that their marriage was made in heaven and may deny any tensions between them. Secondly people may treat an ordinary difficulty, which they may or may not be able to do much about, as a "problem". As Weakland *et al.* comment, "(this second point) appears related to utopian expectations of life. There are countless difficulties of living for which no known ideal or ultimate solutions exist. Even when relatively severe, these are manageable in themselves but can readily become "problems" as a result of a belief that there should or must be an ideal, ultimate solution for them. For instance, there apparently has been a generation gap for the past 5000 years that we know of, but its difficulties only became greatly exacerbated into a "problem" when many people became convinced that it should be closed."[33] Of course what Watzlawick and his colleagues are suggesting is that reality is not an external objective truth. Reality is a relative thing and peoples' views of reality are based on their feelings and belief systems. If people believe family life should be paradise, even minor, normal difficulties will seem like serious failure. This then as we shall discuss in more detail shortly, allows for the possibility of effecting change by altering the meaning situations have for people, by altering their beliefs and feelings about them. One can, of course, imagine that through this process of relabelling or reframing reality people may either be galvanised into responding to situations they have been failing to respond to so far, or they may be helped to become less anxious about situations to which they have been over-reacting so far.

But to return to the *how* of problem development. Weakland *et al.*[34] suggest that "once a difficulty begins to be seen as a 'problem' the continuation, and often the exacerbation of this problem results from the creation of a positive feedback loop, most often centring around those very behaviours of the individuals in the system that are intended to resolve the difficulty: The original difficulty is met with an attempted 'solution' that intensifies the original difficulty, and so on." For example, a parental pair may respond to their daughter's efforts to carve out a more independent life for herself by trying to monitor and control her activities more closely with the result that the daughter becomes resentful and secretive, which serves to increase their vigilance and so on. In other words a spiralling sequence of behaviours develops which results in the escalation of a perhaps ordinary difficulty into a big problem. Thus the parents and their daughter are all "causing" each other to behave as they do, in a circular fashion.

At this point Watzlawick and his colleagues make an interesting distinction between what they call first and second order changes. First order change involves accepting the system and the existing rules as they are and trying to restore functioning through an application of tasks or suggestions which do not demand a change of rules. It would be like saying to someone who was ill, who had been trying one medication without results that he or she should persevere and perhaps take more of the same medicine. Second order change involves changing the rules and hence the system they regulate. A new game replaces the old, as it were, a new approach is tried which involves stepping out of the existing framework. Continuing the analogy of the ill person one might be saying, for instance, "perhaps we have been treating your illness from the wrong angle. Perhaps your current life style needs modifying in order to combat your symptoms", e.g. a different diet, exercise and a new approach to life, rather than drugs to combat high blood pressure. Most common sense, straightforward attempted solutions (like in the example offered in the last paragraph, or when people try to "cheer up" a depressed colleague, or when wives try and draw out their withdrawn, uncommunicative husbands by flooding them with questions and conversation) are what Watzlawick *et al.* would call first order changes. The overall system doesn't change but attempts are made to rectify or maintain the same homeostasis by, for instance, as in the above examples, countering what is seen as problematic by its opposite. Now in many instances such first order changes may be quite appropriate and we regularly employ them as part of the everyday give and take of life. However, in some situations, for instance, at the transitional stress points when a family has to move from one developmental stage to the next, then second order changes which change the system itself are needed. In the example of the overcontrolling parents and their rebellious daughter mentioned above, this family can be described as being at the transitional point between stages 3 and 4 in the Carter and McGoldrick[35] six stage cycle. In this family important changes in their system, involving shifts in peoples' attitudes to each other, in peoples' belief systems about their situation, realignments in relationships and a more open family system boundary are needed to allow for the developmental needs of all three protagonists. Such a change is a second order change. Rules have been changed, a new game is being played. Sometimes, of course, problems arise when people attempt a second order change when a first order change is more appropriate. An example of this is in families with step-parents where step-children are being instructed not only to start behaving according to their step-parents' wishes but also are being "ordered" to like them too. In other words people are demanding changes of attitude and are not content with changes of behaviour. In this context, Maddox's[36] suggestion that in such situations all that step-relatives can demand is politeness can be seen as a much more appropriate first order change.

Given this analysis of how problems typically arise in families it should be becoming clear that it is important to avoid linear thinking when trying to understand what is going on in a given situation. We shall return to this in more detail when we describe our task-centred approach to helping families but it is relevant to explain this briefly here. If one sees a family as a system, as we do, one should seek a "systemic" assessment of problems, looking for "causation" in the circular interactions between family members. Thus in their recent book, Minuchin and Fishman (1981)[37] stress the need to identify circular causes. Instead of just accepting that someone is depressed, for example, one needs to ask oneself, "Who is helping that person to be depressed?" and "How does he or she contribute to their behaving thus?" Similarly one may ask questions on the lines of, "If someone were helping you to be over-involved (or under-involved) with a child, who would it be?", in a situation where such a problem is presented. Such questioning (within oneself and sometimes of family members) underlines the reciprocity of behaviours. A person's behaviour is discussed as "caused by others" and as "causing" others' behaviour. Other examples of such questions might be, "How do you arrange to get your wife to make all the arrangements?" and "How does your wife help you to do this?" Even when problematic children can be reviewed as rejecting complementarity with their families and defending their individuality against the encroachment of the system, it is still true that family members are all causing each other to behave in ways which maintain such children's behaviour.

As we shall go on to elaborate in Chapter 3, Watzlawick and his colleagues adopt a very pragmatic approach to treatment. "We try to base our conceptions and interventions on direct observation in the treatment situation of what is going on in systems of human interaction, *how* they continue to function in such ways and *how* they may be altered most effectively."[38] But first, in Chapter 2, we will define what we believe family therapy aims to accomplish and we will offer some suggestions for when family therapy might be most appropriately employed.

References

1. Pollak, Otto, Social determinants of family behaviour, in E. Younghusband (ed.) *Social work with families*, National Institute Social Services Library No. 4, GAU (1965).
2. Skynner, A. C. R., The minimum sufficient network, in *Social Work Today*, **2**, No. 9 (1971).
3. Pincus, A. and Minahan, A., Social work practice: Model and Method, Illinois, F. E. Peacock Inc. (1973).
4. Walrond-Skinner, S. (ed.), *Family and marital psychotherapy. A critical approach*, London, Routledge and Kegan Paul (1979).

5. Walrond-Skinner, S., *Family therapy. The treatment of natural systems*, Lib. S/W, London, RKP (1976).
6. Skynner, A. C. R., Boundaries, in *Social Work Today*, **5**, No. 10 (1974).
7. Jordan, W., *The social worker in family situations*, Lib. S/W RKP (1972).
8. *Ibid*.
9. Minuchin, S., *Families and family therapy*, Tavistock publications (1974).
10. Kingston, P., The social context of family therapy, in Walrond-Skinner (ed.) *Op Cit.* (1979).
11. Walrond-Skinner, S., *Op. Cit.* (1976).
12. For a much more detailed elaboration on assessing families see Ogden, G. and Zevin, A., *When a family needs therapy*, Beacon Press, Toronto (1976).
13. Minuchin, S., *Op Cit.* (1974).
14. Haley, J., *Problem-solving therapy. New strategies for effective family therapy*, Jossey-Bass Inc. (1976).
15. *Ibid*.
16. Minuchin, S., *Op. Cit.* (1974).
17. Maddox, B., *The half parent: Living with other people's children*, London, Andre Deutsch (1976).
18. Robinson, M., Step-families: A reconstituted family system, in *Journal of Family Therapy*, **2**, No. 1 (Feb.) (1980).
19. Maddox, B., *Op. Cit.*
20. Ireland and Dawes, Working with the client in his family, in *Probation Journal* (Dec.) (1975).
21. Minuchin, S., *Op. Cit.* (1974).
22. Vogel, E. F. and Bell, N. W., The emotionally disturbed child as the family scapegoat, in Vogel and Bell (eds.) *A modern introduction to the family*, Free Press (1960).
23. Walker, C., Some variations in marital satisfaction, in Peel, J. and Chester, R. (eds.) *Equalities and inequalities in family life*, Academic Press (1977).
24. Duvall, E., *Marriage and family development*, 5th. edition, Philadelphia, Lippincott (1977).
25. Carter, E. A. and McGoldrick, M., The family life cycle and family therapy: An overview, in Carter and McGoldrick (eds.) *The family life cycle. A framework for family therapy*, N. Y., Gardner Press Inc. (1980).
26. Scherz, F. H. Theory and practice of family therapy, in Roberts, R. W. and Nee, R. H. (eds.) *Theories of social casework*, Univ. Chicago Press (1970).
27. *Ibid*.
28. Haley, J. *Uncommon therapy: the psychiatric techniques of Milton H. Erickson*, N. Y., Norton (1973).
29. Minuchin, S., *Op. Cit.* (1974).
30. Watzlawick, P., Weakland, J. and Fisch, R., *Change: Principles of problem formation and resolution*, N. Y., W. W. Norton (1974).
31. Weakland, J., Fisch, R., Watzlawick, P., and Bodin, A. M., Brief therapy: focussed problem resolution, in *Family Process*, **13**, 141–168 (1974).
32. *Ibid*.
33. *Ibid*.
34. *Ibid*.
35. Carter, E. A. and McGoldrick, M., *Op. Cit.* (1980).
36. Maddox, B., *Op. Cit.* (1976).
37. Minuchin, S. and Fishman, H. C. *Family Therapy Techniques*, Harvard University Press (1981).
38. Weakland *et al.*, *Op. Cit.* (1974).

CHAPTER 2

Family Therapy—a Method of Work

The Aim of Family Therapy

Given that the ideas outlined in Chapter 1 influence our thinking about families, what do we aim to achieve through the method of family therapy? Basically we try to intervene in and modify those aspects of a family system which are interfering with the management of the life tasks of the family and its members. We focus on the transactional patterns within families and seek to change them so that people will relate to each other differently. We try and increase choices for people by demonstrating that situations may be viewed and tackled differently, that there are other, more productive ways of dealing with each other. We seek to restore or modify the family's structure and functioning by interrupting the sequences of behaviour through which those aspects are expressed and, like Watzlawick, Haley, Minuchin and others we are prepared to use a variety of therapeutic means, tending to use "what seems to work" in a given situation, having to work on the basis of "trial and error" at times.

The above may sound rather ambitious but in fact we try to work towards limited, realistic goals based on the problems presented to us by the family. We believe that nothing breeds like success and anyway even small relief in one area of a family's functioning can make a great deal of difference to the "comfort" of family members. We do not, therefore, aim to restore families to perfect functioning, we are satisfied with limited changes which reduce strain and anxiety and which enable people to enjoy each other a little more. Realistic therapy is, therefore, like aspirin! We use this simile to stress the notion of setting small, achievable goals, but the work is no mere first aid because, very often, apparently small changes can generate a spiral of positive interactions. This is to be expected, of course, given the systems orientation we have towards family dynamics.

We prefer to stick to the "here and now" of situations, focusing on how problems are currently being maintained. Offering insight into the original causes of things often degenerates into games of "who's to blame for this?", which merely serve to put people on the defensive, and even more limited insight-giving, in terms of explaining how problems are being maintained is not always helpful. As we've already indicated people functioning within a

21

system often need help from outside to change things; understanding why things are going wrong does not always enable them to make appropriate changes in the sequences of behaviour of which they are part. Thus we concentrate on how people are behaving towards each other, we attempt to spot and understand the family's usual transactional patterns which we then try to modify in line with the goals agreed with the family. It is not particularly necessary to dwell too long on people's feelings about situations either. As Frank Pittman (1977)[1] remarks "People get bogged down in the complexities of how they feel and begin to think that their feelings have some concrete importance. They forget that what happens to them is determined not so much by how they feel but by what they do. In general, if they do things differently they will feel differently about themselves and other people will treat them differently."

Selecting families—indications and contra-indications for the use of family therapy

There is a mass of literature on this topic, some of it contradictory and hence confusing. It may help if we look at why there are differing views on the subject. Walrond-Skinner[2] comments that family therapy is still at an early stage of development "with practitioners and researchers simply lacking sufficient experience with their subject to be able to offer anything approaching a definite set of conditions for its use." In addition, as she goes on to point out, given that there are so many "sorts" of family therapy, what may seem to be a contra-indication for the method as a whole in fact turns out to be a contra-indication for one particular theoretical and practical application but an indication for another. Beal (1976)[3] found that therapists whose theoretical orientation led them to be particularly concerned with the appropriate expression of emotion in a family were more concerned anyway about indications and contra-indications for family therapy than were therapists who, concerning themselves with systemic, structural and communicational aspects of family life, aimed to change the interactions between people, the ways they behaved towards each other, rather than promoting emotional growth within people.

In seeking to answer the question then about when family therapy is the first choice method of work in a given situation, we have come to the view that there are two parts to the answer which themselves can be put as two separate questions:

1. Should a family assessment be undertaken?
2. Then, is family therapy the treatment of first choice?

As regards the first question, an article by Clarkin, Frances and Moodie (1979)[4] has been quite helpful to us. We have simplified their findings considerably and in the chart below have set out what seem to be the most important criteria for deciding on the advisability (or otherwise) of a family assessment.

Proceed to a Family Assessment?

NO (usually) *IF:*

(a) One or more family members strongly prefer or insist on the privacy of an individual evaluation.

(b) It is particularly important not to undermine a family member's attempts to separate from the family, e.g. a young adult who has recently left home.

(c) The family is breaking up with little or no desire for reconciliation.

(d) The family has a history of sabotaging treatment efforts. Some family therapists would not see this as a contra-indication but as an increased challenge! (Particularly those interested in paradoxical work.)

(e) The presenting individual would not trust someone who has also seen his or her family.

(f) Extreme psychotic episodes are apparent in the identified patient.

YES (usually) *IF:*

1. A child or adolescent is the presenting problem.

2. An individual couple or the whole family is defining the problem as a family issue.

3. The presenting issue is a family or marital problem serious enough to jeopardise family relationships, job stability, health, parenting ability of the adults.

4. There has been a recent family crisis—illness, job loss, death or normal transitional stage in the family life cycle.

5. Psychiatric treatment (especially hospitalisation) is being considered for a family member.

6. Improvement in one individual in the family leads to problems developing in another.

7. Individual or group treatment of an individual is failing *and* the client is involved with family problems *or* needs to have family issues demonstrated *or* family cooperation is needed to allow the client to change.

Barker (1981)[5] provides a thorough summary of methods for undertaking a family assessment. For instance he describes a Triaxial system which focuses on dysfunction in the areas of family development, family subsystems and group aspects of family life. In our co-therapy work such assessment has been undertaken by whoever is referring a family to us though obviously in our planning and during our earliest meetings with a family we are aware of the possibility that the family has been inappropriately referred. Moreover, of course, we need to continue the process of exploring family problems and needs. This brings us to the point that in practice it is not easy to see a separation between assessment and treatment. As many would argue, it is impossible to have an encounter with others without everyone in the meeting being changed in some way. Similarly exploratory interventions often produce change. For example, at the end of a first session with a family we usually suggest an "exploratory task." What the family members do with the task helps us to understand family problems and needs more fully but, of course, if the task is performed then treatment has begun because change has occurred. (Our comments in the next chapter on "problem definition" and "problem exploration" will provide elaboration on our task centred approach to assessment.)

As regards the second question about when family therapy might, on the basis of a family assessment, be the treatment of first choice we have produced another chart based very much on our practical experience and on the theoretical ideas which underpin our work, which we have described earlier.

Proceed to Family Therapy?

NO (usually) *IF:*

(a) There are practical limitations. Family members may be dead, geographically distant or completely unmotivated to engage in any type of therapeutic work.

(b) The situation has been presented too late to offer the family therapist much hope of bringing about constructive change. Salvage of individuals is all that can be achieved.

(c) It becomes clear that people in fact don't want to change. They need the stressful interpersonal situations which initially they (or others) presented as problems, e.g. sado-masochistic relationships.

(d) Certain members of the family need individual help *before* family therapy can be attempted, e.g. because of extreme emotional deprivation, depression, organic illness or other problems.

YES (usually) *IF:*

1. The IP's presenting problems are seen to be expressing the pain or dysfunction of the family system, e.g. an adolescent is acting out in some way, a child's behaviour seems to be expressing something for someone else in the family, a child is being scapegoated in order to take the focus off a difficult marital relationship.

2. Family members are themselves perceiving their difficulties in relationship terms, e.g. parent/child, marital pair, without "throwing up" an identified patient. It may be that such family members are attempting to maintain unrealistically high levels of mutual devotion or symmetry or are functioning under the misapprehension that their in fact normal tensions are abnormal.

3. The evidence suggests that normal difficulties associated with different stages in a family's life

(e) Statutory duties will seriously interfere with attempts to offer family therapy. (Involving another worker, perhaps as a co-worker, often overcomes this kind of problem.)

(f) Where the socio-economic or cultural situation of the family may temporarily or permanently contra-indicate family therapy, e.g. what is maintaining a family's problems can be located in the supra-system; a family's religious or cultural norms may prevent women or children expressing themselves directly.

cycle are being mishandled, often as a result of over or under reaction, e.g. situations where the adult couple in the family have "forgotten" that they have two sub-system relationships to maintain—their *marital* as well as their parental relationship; where parents are not making appropriate allowance for their children's capabilities and needs—parents, for instance, with near adult-like expectations of their pre-school age children's behaviour; where one parent has an overly enmeshed relationship with a child which is excluding the other parent and is suffocating the child (found in some school phobia cases); where the mother has not noticed or does not want to recognise that her children are old enough to want and be expected to take more responsibility for managing themselves and the house, "martyred mother/peripheral father" family situations with adolescent aged children; where an adolescent is not being allowed to "launch" him or herself.

4. There are serious boundary problems within the family, e.g. a child controls or manipulates the parents and may be actively defiant, families with step-parents, three-generational problems.

5. Families exhibiting extreme integrative or centrifugal strains.

6. The family is seriously disorganised and people may be blaming each other for the problems presented. The family exhibits poor

problem-solving capabilities, there are chronic communication problems, people may be behaving in unreliable, inconsistent and impulsive ways, excessive centrifugal tendencies may be apparent.

7. Improvement in one family member leads to deterioration in another.

We think it is important to stress again that a decision to use a family therapy approach does not mean that whole family interviews become obligatory. As we have already stated, when describing the systems orientation to families, work with individuals, sub-systems and/or the whole family may be needed in order to produce changes in the family system. Moreover, one also has to make decisions about whether one needs to see the family on a short term, medium or long term basis and how often one intends to meet with the family. (A number of family therapists suggests that 3/4 week gaps between sessions are optimal as this gives a family time to absorb and digest the content of a session and time to tackle any "homework" that may have been set for them.)

We hope the above offers some guidance as to when we think family therapy may be most productively employed in work with families. In the next two chapters we move on to an elaboration of the theoretical means through which we attempt to achieve our aims as family therapists and to discuss co-therapy work. Then, as previously indicated, in Part II of the book we will show how we *apply* this theory to the practical situation of work with a family.

References

1. Pittman, F., The family that hides together, in Papp, P. (ed.) *Full length case studies*, N.Y. Gardner Press Inc. (1977).
2. Walrond-Skinner, S., Indications and contra-indications for the use of family therapy, in *Journal of child psychology and psychiatry*, **19**, pp. 57–62 (1978).
3. Beal, E. W., Current trends in the training of family therapists, in *American Journal of Psychiatry*, **133**, 137–141 (1976).
4. Clarkin, J. F., Frances, A. J. and Moodie, J. L., Selection criteria for family therapy, in *Family Process*, **18**, No. 4 (1979).
5. Barker, P., *Basic Family Therapy*, Granada, London (1981).

CHAPTER 3

Applying Family Therapy—A Theoretical Model

In this chapter we outline the model and means we use in order to achieve our aims of work with families.

A Task-centred Approach To Family Therapy

Ours is a primarily task-centred approach which draws on the principles outlined in William Reid's book *The Task-centred System* (1978)[1] and on similar ideas and techniques suggested by many family therapists. This approach borrows from problem solving theory and behaviour modification thinking. It is a method which aims to achieve behavioural change in the here and now, rather than insight; a method which sees problems as having a circular causality in the present, rather than a linear causality in the past. Our approach relies heavily on time-limited contracts and on seeing the client system as the primary change agent, through the completion of tasks between sessions. Linked to this, our work includes a strategic approach to family problems, seeing it as our responsibility to manoeuvre the family sub-systems into behaving in such ways as to enable, rather than hinder, satisfactory functioning. We believe that some families are so disturbed in their patterns of interaction that paradoxical methods are necessary for the production of therapeutic change. We will discuss such strategic manoeuvring and the use of paradox later in the chapter but first we will outline the principles of task-centred work.

"Tasks" are actions to be taken by the client system between sessions. (This does not preclude the use of similar activities within sessions, as an aid to assessment, to get people used to working on activities together and to show them how it can be enjoyable.) Task-centred work is a form of guided self-help in which the client system is helped to overcome its problem by its own efforts. This involves a detailed working out of suitable tasks, achieveable by the family between sessions, the completion of which will solve the problem or at least reduce the pain of the situation to a tolerable level. The role of the social worker or therapist is to get the family *doing* and doing the *right* task. To this end, he or she has four main pieces of work to accomplish, i.e. four phases of task-centred work:

(1) *Engagement* This involves careful, thorough self-introduction and a full and repeated explanation of the roles of the worker and the family, of the purpose of the involvement and of the manner of proceeding. Even at this early stage contracts are to the fore, e.g. "let us agree to have two exploratory sessions and we will then decide where to go from there." At the end of the first session an introductory task is proposed, usually of a diagnostic or information gathering nature, e.g. "complete this question-naire before the next session." An example of such a questionnaire will be given in Chapter 6. The engagement session, the first full session with the family includes listening to the family's first account of the problem and encouraging them all to participate in this preliminary discussion of difficul-ties as seen by the various members. Haley (1976)[2] devotes a large section of his book to this first session and we will return to this later in the chapter.

(2) *Definition* This second phase is more specific and·is concerned with fully clarifying what the problem is, what it is that is troubling the client system and what is wanted. This helps with the question of motivation, through showing that one is interested in working towards the satisfaction of *their* wants and not one's own goals. Both families and social workers often have a bad habit of defining problems in vague, unhelpful ways. Problems should, instead, be defined in a quantifiable way, e.g. not "we row a lot over drink," but "I get upset on a Saturday night when my husband comes home drunk. This happens about 3 weeks out of 4." The definition should also include a clear definition of success—what changes the family would settle for.

In defining a problem it is important to make sure that it is a problem acknowledged by the family as theirs, not a problem ascribed to someone else, e.g. not "my husband has a drinking problem" but "we have a problem with my husband's drinking as it's affecting us all." The client is the system which has an acknowledged problem and in this method of working it is by the "client's" own action (changing its functioning) that problems are solved. In working with families, then, it is important to identify members' "dissatisfied wants" and, at this stage, to begin helping them to see that "the problem" is a *common* problem, affecting them all. Even if the problem is one of "Mum being unable to manage the budget" this can be expressed as "disagreement *between us* about money." Problems also need to be defined specifically so that there is some measure (baseline) of their severity and frequency, otherwise progress becomes difficult to assess and success hard to define.

Assessment of the problem situation includes consideration of the *beliefs* of the family members concerning the problem and concerning the obstacles to its solution. It is frequently a task of the worker to modify these beliefs and to relabel or reframe the situation, often as "normal." For example, a child's upsetting behaviour can sometimes be labelled in his hearing as "helpful" in that it prompts the parents to work closer with each other in dealing with family difficulties. Such a definition changes the attitudes of all concerned and allows them to change their behaviour without "losing face." We shall return to this aspect of work later on in the chapter.

Throughout this phase of work one tries to avoid linear causality thinking or seeking explanations for problems in the past. The cause of a problem is that which, here and now, maintains it in existence, i.e. that obstacle or those obstacles which prevent it being solved. Cause is seen in interactional terms—people are reacting to others who, in turn, are reacting to them and the "cause" of a problem is often the effort of one party to solve it. Whatever their original cause, problems persist only if they are maintained by the current behaviour of family members interacting with each other. Therefore we try to assess what behaviour is maintaining the problem and part of our assessment of family problems is seeking out what attempts members have made to deal with their difficulties up to now. The chances are that these efforts are aggravating the situation and tasks will have to be designed to interrupt them and perhaps produce the opposite behaviour in some instances. So we ask not "*why* is he depressed?" but "*what* is happening in his situation and *how* are people affecting each other?"

To get as full an answer as possible to the question, "what is happening?" and to develop some possible answers to "how can change be produced?" we often use symbolic drawings and family sculpts. These will be illustrated in the case presentation in Chapter 7. Suffice it to say at this point that such representations have a number of functions. Firstly they will usually demonstrate that each person in a situation sees that situation differently. Secondly they emphasise the fact that we are looking at "how they are with each other" in the here and now. This focuses family members' minds on the present and gets them away from blaming each other or making comments like "he did so-and-so in the past." Thirdly family dynamics such as coalitions, dominances, closenesses and the breakdown of generational boundaries, which have been briefly described in Chapter 1, are often illustrated in the family's productions.

In drawings families are invited to show how they all are towards each other in terms of closeness by placing their initials or cartoons of themselves on a sheet of paper. Such drawings often tell one a great deal but they are not as informative as sculpts. Families usually enjoy sculpting each other and the method enables them to show the worker and each other quite painful situations without upsetting each other. In family sculpting one member at a time, with some explanatory direction from the therapist, arranges the other family members in a tableau which physically symbolises that member's views of their relationships—how they are in terms of closeness, distance, coalitions etc. Feelings and attitudes can be shown in postures, poses and spacing, showing a snapshot of the family as seen by the sculptor. This picture is worth a thousand words and gives clear spatial expression to confused interactions. The other family members agree to remain silent and to let the sculptor move them about. This cuts out argument, blaming and the smoke-screen of words often encountered. As alliances and conflicts are choreographed (very simply) they are made firm and when the sculpt is complete family members are asked to "freeze" it for a few moments and to ask themselves how it feels. They then sit down and each is asked how he or she felt. This makes clear their individuality as people, while the sculpt, painful as it might have been, heightens the sense of family unity and how each person is an essential part of it. Sculpts of "how we are" can easily be followed by sculpts of "how we would like things to be" and this helps to set goals and even generates the optimism that they are attainable.

The accurate definition of the problem, then, leads logically to a setting of appropriate goals and a consideration of the duration of effort necessary to achieve them. Once the goals are clear, specific and agreed, one is half-way towards selecting and working out tasks to achieve them. In this process the worker may need to challenge "wants" that are unrealisable, and this includes helping people to acknowledge that their wants are really often unending and that, therefore, it is necessary for people to specify what they will settle for here and now.

(3) *Task setting* Here the thinking is also not "why are the problems present" but, "having seen what is happening, how can it be changed?" This is in keeping with the thinking of behaviourists such as Stuart (1975)[3] who says that holding to vertical, causal (or terminal) hypotheses functions as "negative cues for change efforts" and weakens the likelihood of their occurring. In other words, if one sees the problem as "caused" in the past one can become switched off in one's change efforts by the feeling that what is done is done and therefore is unchangeable. Psychodynamic thinking and insight tend to lead to excuses for not changing—"this is how I am, I can't help it, we know why we are like this." We try to work out ways (tasks) that will correct the current, circular, interactional "cause" of the symptomatic behaviour.

Deciding what is to be done to achieve the goals set is, therefore, the third phase of the work. It involves clarifying the goals and, above all, providing a *structure* for the performance of tasks. This structure includes working out tasks for the family that are feasible (achievable by them between sessions). In order to be feasible tasks may need to be incremental, increasing in difficulty only when the family is sufficiently skilled and confident. The structure includes specifying who will do what, when and how and for how long. It may be necessary to teach certain skills, to demonstrate and rehearse them with family members. Selecting tasks can be a collaborative activity, done in full consultation with family members, rather than a technique to be applied to passive subjects. The only exception to this is when paradoxical work is required to overcome the system's resistance. When, however, paradoxical tactics are not required, this phase of work includes encouraging the family, making explicit the rationale behind the effort, providing family members with incentives to persevere, generating various alternatives from which they can choose, showing optimism and confidence in their ability and refining task contracts patiently until they are to everybody's satisfaction.

In families it is important to set tasks which will upset the rut in which their interaction is stuck and which will stop the behaviour that is maintaining the problem in existence. Such tasks may be for individuals, pairs or groups and there are two main types. Firstly there are "straight" tasks which may have a variety of purposes—(a) exploratory, (b) problem-solving, e.g. working on a budget, (c) conversational— to improve communication, (d) enjoyable— to upset a negative, hostile rut, and (e) reward-earning—bringing an agreed response, e.g. if a child behaves well he is taken to the cinema. Secondly there are paradoxical tasks, which will be discussed later on in this chapter. (Appendix A contains a list of facilitative exercises that may be useful as tasks from time to time.) In this phase of work the role of the worker can be described as that of negotiator-cum-coach.

Restructuring is an important aspect of task work. In families where there are confused generational boundaries, with the parents over-involved in the children system, or with a "parental-child" intruding into the parental system then tasks may be especially useful. One suggestion might be to focus on the management of household tasks within the family, as a way of realigning things. It might be necessary to spend a good deal of time, possibly in several sessions, working out a "fair sharing" of these routine tasks, the family chores. One's fairness in this exercise encourages them to treat each other fairly. Family chores are closely related to family roles and a change in chores-management can bring about a change of relationships by untangling inappropriate cross-generational roles. In another example, in families where there is a "peripheral father" who leaves everything to his wife to sort out and where the wife is overinvolved in her maternal role and is treating grown-up children as babies, it is essential to get "fair shares" that involve everyone in sharing what the mother is now overburdened with, so that she can be free to attend to herself and to her spouse role. As she moves closer to her husband the marital and parental coalitions are underlined, their boundaries are firmed up and some space is made between them and the children so that they too can grow more freely. This work involves going into detail about who does such chores as shopping, cooking, cleaning, washing, dusting, making beds. (It is not unusual to find a worn-down mother spending hours collecting up clothes to be washed and searching under beds for the used socks of her grown-up sons, as well as doing a job outside the home.

Additional structural tasks can be suggested to emphasise the separateness of their sub-systems in cases of over-enmeshed families. Minuchin (1974)[4] talks of "mapping" the family coalitions so as to plan tasks that will restructure the family and transform dysfunctional transactional patterns. This can involve physically separating parents and children by simply asking to see parents on one occasion and the children on another, requesting that those not being seen are not present. This usually compels the parents to go out together while one meets the children; it gives both groups a sense of separate identity.

We often use the technique of asking the parents to go into a separate room to work out a solution to a disagreement between the children. We find the disagreement often ends when the parents leave the room where the children are, because the children no longer have an "audience" and the fact of their parents leaving "upsets" the usual sequence of events. They are left wondering, "what will Mum and Dad decide?" Meanwhile Mum and Dad are advised to return with an agreed decision, a united front which affirms their coalition. Further joint tasks can be given to the parental pair to emphasise the separateness of their system, e.g. having an evening out together or shopping together.

(4) *Review of task implementation* (feedback and consolidation). This takes place after each set of tasks, or contract, has been completed. Where "straight" tasks are used, it involves providing family members with encouragement, praise, warm constructive feedback; where paradoxical tasks are used, one responds with surprise, suspicion, guarded scepticism and doubt at the "unexpected" result. The reason for this latter response will be explained later. The experience of even the slightest success is important— one is aiming to provide the family with a constructive problem-solving experience. Nothing succeeds like success, especially when it comes through one's own efforts. The emphasis on feedback is close to that used in behaviour modification and the use of time limits helps to heighten the optimism and motivation. Where tasks are complex or involve several people it is helpful to design a simple record along these lines, as in Reid (1978):[5]

Who does it?	What will be done?	When?	How did it go?
Mr. X Mrs. X John Anne	Wash up	Nightly	

The task-centred method of intervention holds to the core conditions of effective counselling, accurate empathy, genuineness, non-possessive warmth, unconditional positive regard and immediacy; it adds to these the structure of problem definition, task selection and time limited contracts. It is most effective in psychosocial difficulties that reflect a relatively recent breakdown in coping ability though we believe it can be effective in even apparently chronic, dysfunctional situations. (See Chapter 2 on selection.) The method's aim is to reduce problems to a tolerable level for the family. However, it is no mere "first aid" since limited, achievable work can have "ripple" effects in terms of making for major attitude change in families and in terms of enhancing a family's general problem-solving capacities.

The First Session

In our work we rely a good deal on the ideas of Jay Haley (1963[6] and 1976[7]). He lays particular emphasis on the first family session and the need to get this right. He breaks the first session down into four parts.

(1) *The social meeting* The worker introduces him/herself and observes what the family, by its very seating and leadership, is showing about itself and what illustrations of its problems it is giving. This part of the session ends with stating some ground rules about confidentiality, about no recriminations after sessions, about everyone having a right to be heard, about people having different views on things, about no one speaking for anyone else and about the right of everyone to disagree with the therapist.

(2) *Problem exploration* "Getting down to business." The worker asks what is happening and how the family wants things to be. If disagreements are shown, so that arguments develop, one stops them by saying that "we will return to that point later." The therapist is "in charge" and very much responsible for the session. Unspoken conflict is listened for, e.g. when complaining about her child, is a mother really complaining about her husband? While problems are usually put in terms of one person the worker's task to to look at them in terms of more than one person—if possible, in terms of the whole family, e.g. "Our son is disobedient" may mean "we can't agree among ourselves about our son's disobedience." As the therapist, one should ask oneself, "what is happening in the whole situation that makes the problem exist and persist?" However, one accepts the family's account of the situation and one does not offer insights or interpretations. For example, when parents complain of a son's behaviour as a problem we do not say "your son is not the real problem it is your spouse relationship that is the cause of the trouble" (if we think that there *are* problems in that sub-system) but, accepting their definition of the problem, we may add "this is a problem for you all, affecting you all." One often finds signs of stress in other family members and one can include these as part of the overall "family problem."

(3) *Interaction or Enactment* This means getting various members of the family to talk with each other about the family problem and to show how

they deal with each other—thereby, it is hoped, they will show their usual sequences and rules of behaviour. As Minuchin and Fishman (1981)[8] point out, although the person *is* his own dance, when a family joins therapy the members control what they present. So, to release sequences beyond such control, they are invited to interact. For instance, a father is asked to control his son who is disturbing the meeting. The accustomed "rules" of interaction usually take over. Enactment therefore means "dance in my presence." Observing the current interactions helps one to consider alternative ways of interacting, all of which contributes to the search for a solution. Enactment widens the focus—the family has usually narrowed its focus on to "the problem member" and other members fail to show their own contribution and how it maintains the situation; enactment shows one how they do contribute. Therefore enactment improves information gathering, challenges the family's ideas about the problem and also provides a "language" on which to base alternatives. Enactment enables one to experience a family's reality, which will obviously help one to be more effective in selecting tasks which will assist that family to change. Later on, enactment can be a way of providing members with the experience of competence. For example, a parent may be enabled to experience taking appropriate charge over a child within a session, supported by advice and encouragement from the therapist.

Another approach involves asking people about how they think other family members relate to each other. This is Selvini Palazzoli's[9] method of triangular questioning. For example, this could involve asking Mum about how Dad gets on with their son, then asking Dad how Mum gets on with the boy. Or again one could ask various members whether the son is more helpful than the daughter, or the daughter more helpful than the mother and so on. In the end one weaves a full pattern of the family by focusing on criss-crossing triads of people within the family. This brings out many differences of opinion and these are more revealing than what they agree about. Since we do often wonder if the basic problem is a marital one leading to a child being scapegoated and since one cannot here ask this question directly, or ask a child how Mum gets on with Dad, the answer to this dreaded question can be reached by the criss-crossing method. One can ask Mum how Dad gets on with his son, then ask Dad how Mum gets on with the boy and then by asking the other children similar questions and noting the differences and contradictions in their accounts one can "tease out" how the marital pair deal with eath other. In this part of the meeting one watches for overlap of the generational boundaries (systems) as, for example, when one parent sides with a child against the other parent or a grandparent sides with a child against a parent or an older child has become a "pseudo-parent" who bosses the other children.

Having begun to set the baseline of the problem (how bad it is) before treatment begins one moves on to the final part of the session. (The baseline is, in fact, usually not fully clear until the end of the second or third session.)

(4) *Defining change* Here the worker is asking what the family wants from therapy, moving towards a tentative formulation of goals and the allocation of a preliminary task to maintain the momentum that brought the family to join this first session.

Haley's first two phases of the first session reflect those of Reid's phases of Engagement and Definition. Of course there is only a beginning of tentative exploratory tasks and there is no task review in the first session.

In subsequent sessions one works towards a fuller assessment of family interaction, attempted solutions and vicious circles. However, we do not say that no intervention must be attempted or no task prescribed until there is a full understanding. As we have mentioned in Chapter 2, at the end of the first session an exploratory task can be assigned and this can be seen as "exploratory treatment" (Scherz (1970)).[10] This gets the family used to doing "homework" between sessions and it keeps the therapy in their minds, while encouraging family responsibility for working out problems. While (as we will be going on to describe) we use the technique of relabelling, which, in some cases, can be sufficient treatment in itself, we see tasks as central in our work in most cases. As Haley says, learning to change involves doing.

Selvini Palazzoli *et. al.* (1980)[11] advocate having an early hypothesis (based on the referral details) in one's mind and seeking evidence in the first session to prove or disprove it. (An example of an hypothesis would be "the child is being scapegoated because of an unsatisfactory marriage.") If the hypothesis stands up, well and good, if not, then another hypothesis must be formulated. (For instance, the hypothesis might be reformulated as "the trouble is due to anxiety about someone leaving the family"—a developmental stage problem.) Selvini Palazzoli and her colleagues suggest that this gives direction to one's questioning and prevents a disorderly "going round in circles and getting nowhere." This is a particularly useful technique in the first session but it can be useful in subsequent sessions. Our plans for sessions are based on the hypotheses we have generated. For instance, if on the basis of referral information we speculate that the boundaries between the family sub-systems are not clearly enough defined we would plan to explore this in our initial session with a family. If evidence emerges that the parental sub-system is weak and that indeed a child has intruded inappropriately to take over parental functions then our hypothesis would be supported and we would proceed on the basis of this understanding. However, the evidence may not support this hypothesis but suggest other difficulties which we would then hypothesise about and test out in subsequent work with the family.

Positive Connotating: Relabelling: Reframing

Selvini Palazzoli *et. al.* (1978)[12] describe their approach to a family in the following way. They begin by putting a positive connotation on all the problem behaviours within the family. For example, they may say, "all your efforts are due to a desire to keep the family together." This is paradoxical in the sense of being the opposite of the family's "truth" and it paves the way for paradoxical injunctions (or prescriptions) which we will discuss shortly. By thus approving the family's efforts, the therapists are able to "join" the family, a family which is now unable to keep the therapists out of their "game" or to spin them off (like a fairground ride) because the therapists are suggesting the system should continue as before. The therapists run with the system and so are able to join it. (When we say "join" we mean "engage" with the family that is resisting change not, of course, joining in with their circular games.) Haley's view is that when we accept behaviour we inevitably get some control over it. The confirmation, by the therapist, of the "ongoing" situation has two effects. Firstly it makes all the members of it complementary to the system itself and this reduces tension between them (by making them all subservient to the family itself the power struggle between them is eased). Secondly it makes all the family members complementary to the therapist who has implicitly taken the lead by telling them to continue. These two pieces of complementarity contribute to a new symmetry between family members. An authority that approves implies that it has no doubt about its leadership and it is impossible to disqualify that authority since it is confirming the homeostatis of the system. But the family is trapped by a further thought. "If we are so good," the family may think to itself, "why do we need a therapist?"—a question which jolts them and triggers a capacity to change.

Haley too tends to favour putting a positive label on symptomatic behaviour in order to undermine a family's typical labelling process and to alter their beliefs about each other. So "nagging" might be redefined as "trying to reach people," an "avoiding husband" might be described as "a sensitive man avoiding conflict," a "disorganised and irresponsible wife" might become "a lady with feminine characteristics" (no offence to females!), "aggression" might be relabelled "disappointment" or "meaning well but using the wrong methods." In their most recent books, Haley (1980)[13] and Madanes (1981)[14] argue that "bad" behaviour on the part of a child has an essentially protective function in a family system, in that family members can stabilise their interactions with each other around the problematic youngster. Thus even "bad" behaviour can be positively described. By relabelling behaviour in positive terms one is implicitly encouraging it. In this way one has a better chance of achieving change later. Meanwhile, one gives other members of the family a model of how not to be provoked by the behaviour into futile solutions which aggravate it. When faced with highly provocative behaviour, one does not respond to it, one simply describes it. This breaks a fundamental family "rule" about "not defining the rules." When challenged to do something about the problem one takes charge by putting the family in charge and saying "you are the best people to solve the problem," thus avoiding a power struggle with the family which would result in no progress, perpetuating their sad game. Relabelling does not require overt behaviour change or any active co-operation. If one's redefinition of the situation is not openly challenged the behaviour will have already been altered in that its meaning and effect will have been changed (Weakland *et al.* (1974)).[15]

Obviously positive connotating and relabelling behaviour are ways of meeting and overcoming family resistance to change. Minuchin (1974)[16] describes 3 other ways in which resistance may be dealt with, both at the beginning and later on in treatment. Firstly "maintenance" involves supporting the structural status quo of the family sufficiently at times where change is occurring which is making family members feel so anxious and threatened that they may pull out of treatment. For example, in a family where the unequal power sharing between the marital pair is the main focus of work the previously overcontrolling partner may need to be supported and "colluded" with temporarily in order to keep him or her engaged in the work. In other words, one paces progress according to people's capacity to cope with it. Secondly in "tracking" one goes along with a family's efforts to deal with something or someone in principle because their efforts indicate motivation to change and a healthy desire to be actively involved in finding their own solutions, even though one would not have advised what they are actually doing. So one supports the family's intentions, whilst at the same time suggesting different means to achieving their goals. Rather than saying unhelpfully "I don't think you are tackling this the right way" (which often makes people feel defensive and irritated) one can say things like "You've really thought or done a great deal on this. Have you also considered the possibility of . . . ?," or "Yes, and . . ." Thirdly "mimesis" involves adjusting one's style of work and the manner of expressing oneself verbally and nonverbally to the family's style and cultural norms, not in a patronising way but so as to help get alongside them, nearer their "wave-length" so as to speak. (We notice that in their latest book Minuchin and Fishman (1981)[17] now frequently put a positive connotation on the behaviour of each family member, in order to upset the current system by providing new, confusing information.)

Paradoxical Work

As we have already indicated, positive connotating and relabelling behaviour in positive terms are essential ingredients in the formulation of paradoxical tasks or injunctions, to which we would now like to turn our attention. These offer "uncommonsense" ways of tackling difficult family dynamics that render some situations resistant to change, vicious circles that are maintaining problems. The concept of paradox is highly complex and we do not presume in this book to teach inexperienced readers how to fully employ paradoxical interventions. Indeed, many would argue that they are not to be tried out by beginners. While agreeing that beginners should not attempt paradoxical work at the level that, for instance, Selvini Palazzoli and her colleagues do, we believe that an elementary understanding of paradox is useful to social workers faced with families who are adept at defeating attempts to help them. If this understanding only takes the workers as far as offering positive reframes of people's behaviour, this alone often helps. It is our view that anyway paradoxical interventions should only be used sparingly. Straight interventions and tasks should be tried first and it is only when these are repeatedly defeated by the family system that paradoxical man-oeuvres should be considered as a possible strategy. Even then the worker needs to be clear and confident about the rationale behind their use and to have carefully worked out the precise intervention to be offered. Obviously consultation with a colleague or a support group is essential in such instances and we believe that the availability of a co-worker can be very helpful. Given the above provisos, we think that qualified workers might cautiously consider this kind of task-centred work.

To elaborate on paradoxical work, in Chapter 1 the principle of homeostasis was mentioned and the stubbornness of many problems in dysfunctional families. These situations seem to bring out an apparent "cussed" streak in people who are tangled up in a power struggle and who cannot let go for fear of losing face. To suggest they make changes or behave in new ways can easily be counterproductive and can lead to a "digging in of heels" and doing the opposite to what is suggested. Such families, accustomed to disqualifying each other, tend to disqualify any attempt to change them; therefore one can only get to grips with their system by going along with it. If one struggles against such clients they strive all the more to "thwart" the therapist. To counter this, "strategic therapists" use paradoxical prescriptions (injunctions or tasks) in which the problem behaviour (symptom) is encouraged rather than discouraged. This traps the family in a "therapeutic double-bind": if they reject the injunction they are changing and if they accept it they are co-operating with the change agent. This changes the "rules" for them and makes them more amenable to later suggestions.

Cade (1980)[18] states that for paradoxical prescriptions to work, the following conditions are necessary—(a) a context that is identified with change, where there have been preliminary discussions about what change is wanted and what would be acceptable, where change is implicit in ongoing contact; (b) a clear definition of the problem and an understanding of the sequence of behaviours that maintain it in existence; (c) a reframing of the problem behaviour in positive terms; and, finally, (d) a request for the behaviour to continue for the time being, this request being made in the context of concern for the family.

When change does occur it is responded to paradoxically, with caution and scepticism and a suggestion that it is happening too quickly. This traps the family in a further "therapeutic double-bind"—they can only disqualify the worker by maintaining the change. While they may thank the worker and give him or her credit, the worker must not accept such praise. The credit must be the family's—if the worker accepts it the family will set about disqualifying him or her by relapsing! One can say, "I may have pointed you in certain directions but I have no special magic—it was yourselves who spontaneously behaved in this way."

This approach links nicely with the ideas of Watzlawick and others which we have already mentioned in Chapter 1. Repeating their ideas briefly, they suggest that problems are often compounded by the attempts that have been made to solve them and that, therefore, it is a matter of persuading people to ease off and even do the opposite of what they have been trying. The trouble is, when a solution fails to work, people tend to try "more of the same", like two people leaning out of the opposite sides of a boat to balance it—the more the one leans out the more the other has to lean out. To correct it they must do the seemingly contradictory thing of leaning out less—as one leans out less, the other has to respond by leaning out less also. Thinking of the example, mentioned in Chapter 1, of the daughter and the vigilant parents, it seemed that the more they increased their vigilance the more deceptive the daughter became and they all became stuck in that rut by their own "rules". A change of rules, a new game, should be advocated, involving what Watzlawick calls "second order change". More of the same vigilance would be first order change. Of course one could attempt a direct intervention with the family which would involve explaining the needs of adolescents for greater independence and self-responsibility and the fact that the parents needed to modify both their attitudes to and ways of handling their daughter. Straight tasks could be suggested which would serve to reduce their vigilance and her rebellion. This direct approach might work and all well and good if it does. However, given the tendencies of families to resist change and of family members to get "locked" into dysfunctional sequences of behaviour and given some families' urges to thwart their therapists' best efforts, paradoxical injunctions may be needed. In the case of the parents and their daughter, the parents' overcontrolling and vigilant behaviour could be reframed as genuine concern. The parents could be asked to keep observing their daughter's behaviour closely, watching out also for any small glimmers of good behaviour. Their daughter would be advised not to change her behaviour since that would spoil the therapy by giving a false picture of the situation! This would have the effect of relaxing both parents and daughter, of jolting them off their vicious circle and of allowing them to change a little, setting up a positive feedback loop, while "saving face" for them all.

Another example we recently heard of involved a married couple where the husband was very controlling of his wife who was reacting with depression and helpless behaviour. His behaviour was positively relabelled as "being like a mother" and her's as "adolescent rebellion". It was suggested that they should both continue to play out these roles and that the wife needed to behave in childish, acting out ways as she had been doing in order to support her husband. As one might imagine the wife was challenged to thwart not only the therapist's injunction to stay the same but also her husband's efforts to play mother! Peggy Papp[19] stresses that it is important to connect all, or as many as possible of the family members into a circular definition of the problem (a systemic assessment) before prescribing that they continue to be as they are. If a child's misbehaviour, for example, keeps his mother's marital dissatisfaction focused away from father, the mother can be told that it is important to continue to express her disappointment through her son. She can be advised that if she directs it at father it could depress him, her son is more resilient and he should continue to attract this attention. The father should also be complimented for his co-operation in all this. In such a way they are all tied in to the prescription. One does not just ask the son to continue misbehaving as he has, nor the father to be disengaged—the paradox is aimed at the whole familial sequence.

Selvini Palazzoli *et al.*[20] suggest that when some small questionable improvement is reported (as a result of a family trying less hard to continue the old games, trying less to deal with each other in ways that perpetuated the problem) which leads to the family requesting termination of treatment this should be accepted as a spontaneous decision on their part. No question should be raised about how real the improvement is or how wise their request to stop treatment. Instead the workers should suggest that since the agreed number of sessions has not been completed, the contract should be honoured by keeping therapy available should the family decide to continue at a later date. Either the family agrees, saying that the situation is now tolerable or the family may not agree and ask for more sessions immediately. (In going along with a request for an end to treatment, one may negotiate a "follow-up" session if one thinks there is an element of "flight into health".) However, if they ask for more sessions an interval of about four weeks is suggested by the workers who may prescribe a family task for them to attempt in the meantime! This is all very contradictory but playing it "straight" will not bring change in some disturbed families, where straight counselling has probably been tried over and over again, without success. Of course, as we've already emphasised, we will always try direct, straight interventions first and in practice we find that paradoxical work forms only a small part of our actual interventions, though we may consider family dynamics from more lateral, paradoxical angles in order to make sense of them.

While we acknowledge this approach is manipulative and devious, we would argue that this is justifiable. Influence is an inherent element in any form of client-worker contact—it may be less obvious in some forms of work than it is in this type of work and hence easier to deny but that may make it more insidious and more open to abuse. We see two safeguards in our work. We work only with a situation that is acknowledged by the family to be painfully unsatisfactory and we work only towards achieving aims that have been agreed with the family. Then, having assessed the interactions that are contributing to the problem, we proceed to manoeuvre the family in such a way as to allow their system to change in a way that will achieve their aims— namely a less painful family life.

The paradoxical approach, going along with the symptom rather than trying to stop it, is compared by Saposnek (1980)[21] with the approach of the judo artist and the methods by which he manoeuvres his opponent. Looked at in this way, the following points can be drawn out—(1) extension—the worker goes with the momentum of the client and extends his behaviour until he is off balance, e.g. "I can see why you are depressed, you have good reason, but I want you to let yourself go and feel a little more depressed"; (2) pre-empting—being a step ahead of the next move, e.g. "you will probably think I'm stupid but . . ."; (3) lightness of touch—the paradoxical is humorous—client and worker can share a smile and often have a laugh about things; (4) the unexpected (contradiction)—as a judo player puts himself down to unbalance the other so too can one say "I'm not sure I can help—this is a new one on me" and then proceed to deal with the problem; and (5) puzzlement— being amazed at what another is doing and suggesting he or she is changing too quickly—"slow down" or even suggesting he or she try having a relapse (to get it over with!). We came across a lovely example of paradoxical work in a recent article (1980)[22] where two parents brought their little girl in for treatment of the child's severe temper tantrums. The worker relabelled these as an "important means of communication" and therefore to be kept but he suggested that the family should designate part of the house as "the tantrum area" (a dining room or bathroom were possibilities). The child was to be allowed to have temper tantrums, but only in this special area. If the family was out the child would have to wait until they got home to have a tantrum. When the family later reported a big decrease in the number of tantrums the worker expressed a certain amount of concern and suggested that as the tantrums were important the parents should be sure to invite the little girl to have tantrums in her special area. (This strategy was combined with other work to help the little girl develop her vocabulary and ability to express himself in words, using the parents as stimulators and rewarders.)

What About Insight?

In our method one avoids the psychodynamic type of intervention, which is aimed at giving insight. Even when one is discussing drawings and sculpts one is merely looking at their various portrayals of how they see things, one is not suggesting why things are so. If one comments at all, it should be to redefine the interactions in positive terms, as mentioned earlier, to reframe what is happening so as to change their beliefs about it. Cade (1980)[23] gives an example of a difficult son who is causing great stress at home. Ignoring the boy, the therapist assured the parents that his *childish* behaviour was *common* in children who were afraid to grow into adults and that such children should not be hurried or they became more fearful and childish. While sympathising with the parents, the therapist said the son would make the move to "responsible, adult behaviour" at about this time *but* only when he was ready and not before. The parents were advised to help each other to be patient and understanding and careful not to demand responsible behaviour before the son was ready, but to understand that his *fear* was causing him to behave as if he were big and tough. Meanwhile they were asked to watch for the change, as it could come quickly and could be easily missed! This reframing allowed for a more adaptive range of behaviours from all concerned; it brought confusion and doubt that helped to jolt them out of their rut. This kind of "interpretation" looks like an attempt to impart insight, but it is not. It was an attack on their beliefs, designed to undermine the reactions of the adults to their son, as well as provoking the son to behave differently. Once the relabelling was accepted by them, the meaning and effect of the behaviour had already been altered.

Concluding Comments

Before summing up this section we would like to offer the following general *don'ts* with regards to one's intervention efforts:
1. Don't make a power struggle explicit or one risks solidifying it. Rather than discussing the power issue as such, discuss a family's "rules".
2. Don't take sides *consistently*. One may, however, temporarily join various coalitions in order to unsettle their steady state or one may be briefly supportive to different members of a family.
3. Don't seek to give insight.
4. Don't criticise. Instead put positive connotations on behaviours.
5. Don't seek feelings for their own sake and don't be too curious about past history or other problems that are not one's business.
6. Don't forbid the symptomatic behaviour—rather encourage it for the time being.
7. Don't accept credit for change or progress—tell family members they

have behaved spontaneously. The encouragement of the problem can be taken even further on occasions and the behaviour, especially if the person says he or she cannot help it, can be ordered or an increase prescribed. Cade (1980)[24] offers an interesting example of a woman who was unable to enter shops without being ill. He took her to various shops and 'ordered' her to be ill, so that he could see the symptom before beginning to treat it. Several attempts were made until she found that she had visited several shops without being ill.

Haley (1976)[25] has an interesting comment to make about the therapist's style. He believes that one needs to be confident and "sure" about what one is doing, whilst at the same time presenting an "unsure" style to the family. The therapist should show a certain tentativeness which draws out the family's cooperation. We need to be sure enough to take responsibility for the session but unsure enough, in another way, in order to elicit some initiative from the family members. Our style is also quite directive in that we take deliberate action to change the patterns of interaction as powerfully and effectively as possible, using whatever seems to work best. This may involve, however, making suggestions and requesting changes indirectly or implicitly. One way of doing this is to suggest that family members may not yet be ready to change. One might preface one's task suggestion with, "It is probably too soon for you to attempt this but eventually you might be able to . . ."

By way of conclusion, we refer to Weakland *et al.*[26] who also work on the basis that difficult behaviour in one member reflects a dysfunction in the system. Therefore they maneouvre the system. This does not mean seeking a fundamental change in it, in order to get change—even minor changes in people's behaviour can set progressive developments in motion. One aims to read the vicious circle and then substitute a new pattern of behaviour to break it. This often means reversing the usual "solution" being used by the family. Finally these writers recommend us to "think small", i.e. to accept small change, finish the work early and get out while you're winning.

In our work, described in this book, we rely on two planks to stop the family from disqualifying our change effort. Firstly success brings its own rewards—if a family is functioning better, with less pain, as a result of performing their tasks, this improvement will be self-rewarding and attractive. Secondly when change occurs we adopt the guarded, sceptical, paradoxical attitude described above.

To sum up the theory behind our method, we use a task-centred approach which is sufficiently flexible to include the ideas of Haley, Watzlawick, Weakland and others who make use of paradoxical methods in work with disturbed families. In the case we present we will show some modest use of these methods, as well as the use of co-therapy, which we will discuss in the next chapter.

Applying Family Therapy

References

1. Reid, W. J., *The task-centred system*, Columbia Univ. Press (1978).
2. Haley, J., *Problem solving Therapy*, Jossey Bass Inc. (1976).
3. Stuart, R. B., Behavioural remedies for marital ills, in Thompson and Dockens (eds.) *Application of behaviour modification*, Academic Press (1975).
4. Minuchin, S., *Families and Family Therapy*, Tavistock Pubs. (1974).
5. Reid, W. J., *Op. Cit.* (1978).
6. Haley, J., *Strategies of Psychotherapy*, Grune and Stratton (1963).
7. Haley, J., *Op. Cit.* (1976).
8. Minuchin, S. and Fishman, H. C., *Family Therapy Techniques*, Harvard University Press (1981).
9. Selvini Palazzoli, M. S. *et al.*, Hypothesising, circularity, neutrality: Three guidelines for the conduct of the session, in *Family Process*, **19**, 3–12 (1980).
10. Scherz, F. H., Theory and practice of Family Therapy, in Roberts, R. W. and Nee, R. H. (eds.), *Theories of social casework*, Univ. Chicago Press (1970).
11. Selvini Palazzoli, M. S. *et al.*, *Op. Cit.* (1980).
12. Selvini Palazzoli, M. S. *et al.*, *Paradox and counterparadox*, Aronson (1978).
13. Haley, J., *Leaving Home*, McGraw Hill (1980).
14. Madanes, C., *Strategic Family Therapy*, Jossey-Bass (1981).
15. Weakland *et al.*, Brief therapy: Focussed Problem resolution, in *Family Process*, **13**, 141–168 (1974).
16. Minuchin, S., *Op. Cit.* (1974).
17. Minuchin, S. and Fishman, H. C., *Op. Cit.* (1981).
18. Cade, B., Strategic Therapy, in *Journal of Family Therapy*, **2**, 89–99 (1980).
19. Papp, P., in Minuchin, S. and Fishman, H. C., *Op. Cit.* (1981).
20. Selvini Palazzoli *et. al.*, *Op. Cit.* (1978).
21. Saposnek, D. T., Aikido: A model for brief strategic therapy, in *Family Process*, **19**, 3 (1980).
22. Breunlin, D., Jones, H. and Packer, A., Therapist style in family therapy: Two contrasting studies, in *Family Therapy or Family Therapies?*, Barnardo Social Work Papers No. 9 (1980).
23. Cade, B., *Op. Cit.*
24. *Ibid.*
25. Haley, J., *Op. Cit.* (1976).
26. Weakland, J. *et al.*, *Op. Cit.* (1974).

CHAPTER 4

Co-therapy and Work with Families

As will be seen from the case presentation in Part II, we work as a co-therapy pair, meeting the family together and sharing each session. We acknowledge that this is not the only way of working. Many therapists prefer to work alone in sessions with families and indeed personal experience indicates that our approach can be employed, with minor adaptations, by a solo therapist. We acknowledge that there are critics of co-working and we accept that suitable partners may not always be available. Beginners may feel there is much pressure involved in working in a team, interviewing under the critical eye of a frank colleague. One could feel exposed and under pressure to be "highly professional". Whitaker (1972)[1] says that co-therapy poses even a more fundamental challenge in that it challenges the very person of the therapist, not just his style. We believe, however, that the pressures can be dealt with and they are far outweighed by the benefits of a partnership. Of course it is important to select a co-therapist with whom one can feel comfortable, and Rice's research (1972)[2] showed that effectiveness was related to the degree of comfort in the relationship between the therapists. We feel this comfort is not only necessary in the sessions but also afterwards, when we need an open frankness in assessing how things went, how well we co-operated and "counterpointed", a term we will explain shortly.

There are many ways in which workers differ from each other—age, sex, colour, qualification, theoretical orientation and so on. Consequently the possible combinations within co-therapy pairs are many. In our experience most co-worker pairs comprise a man and a woman with roughly similar training and experience and complementary styles of work. However, we also know of other co-worker pairs where such is not the case—same sex pairs; pairs where one worker is far more experienced in family therapy than the other or where one is trained and the other is not, (e.g. a probation officer working with a volunteer); pairs involving workers from different disciplines, (e.g. a social worker in combination with a community psychiatric nurse). Whatever the combinations it is crucial that co-worker teams should give themselves time to work out mutual expectations and understandings. In addition they need to consider what image they are likely to present to a family, what models they will be offering of, for instance, power-sharing and sex role behaviour. While the first tendency when working with a partner is to worry about achieving sufficient co-operation, the other extreme is a possibility, i.e. having a pair who become an "ego mass", unable to disagree and huddled together in the icy blast of the family's onslaught. Walrond-Skinner (1976)[3] warns against this and says it heightens the pain of the family which is thus excluded and made to feel like children whose parents are unable to allow them into their relationship. As with effective parents, competition and disagreements between co-workers should not become issues if there is adequate opportunity for frank discussion.

To elaborate on its benefits, we find co-therapy to be a speedy, effective and supportive way of working. It ensures thorough assessment, so necessary in complex, rigid, difficult families; it ensures detailed planning of sessions: it brings a definite structure to the work, so vital with the many cases that can be described as chaotic; it provides security and a life-line that prevents one being sucked into endless circular arguments; it shows the family a model of shared authority by a pair able to give each other confirmation and it helps focus the work on interactional change within the family now, avoiding transferences and projective identifications as much as possible.

Each of these advantages will be discussed but first we wish to comment on the style or climate of the relationship that develops between a co-therapy pair and a family. Meeting a family as a pair appears to underline the group aspect, where individuals do not feel so pin-pointed or blamed; the meeting becomes more of an "occasion", cups of tea are usually offered, the family feels free to ask us personal questions and we are treated like a pair of family relatives. (*NB* Our sessions are usually held in the family home; we have no large interview room or one-way mirror.) One might think that meeting a pair might be more threatening than meeting one therapist but, paradoxically, people seem to be less threatened; they quite naturally take to addressing us by our first names. Perhaps this relaxed atmosphere is partly due to the therapists feeling more confident; we tend to think that by undertaking to work as a pair we have already accepted that our "errors" are "exposed"; we are quite philosophical about errors and even believe that they can be advantageous. (This point has been discussed in the introduction.) We assume that families will be resistant to change and will fear it, therefore we are determined to be active, persistant, explicit and direct in our efforts. Mueller *et al.* (1976)[4] says these qualities are necessary, as well as a "powerful, committed and optimistic orientation" towards the family. This helps the family to persist through the very threatening process of change and somehow the feeling of determination and security in the therapist pair rubs off on the family. We are usually introduced to a family by a member of a social work agency, as "specialists" in this work and we deliberately use this credibility to further the orientation described by

Mueller. (We stress that the relaxed cosiness described above does not seem to block us from moving quickly on to business after ten minutes or so of social chat and cups of tea.)

Elaborating on the advantages we listed above, we find that two heads are better than one in overcoming, within a friendly, family-relative-type relationship, resistance to change. Progress appears to be much more rapid than with single worker efforts. This, however, is not new—Adler used co-therapy in his clinic in Vienna where children were found to respond better to two theologists rather than to one alone. The support one gets from a co-therapist is bound up with the advantages of joint assessment and planning. Working with someone leads more quickly to a clearly defined analysis of the problem which in turn clarifies the purpose of the involvement and leads to the development of specific aims for each meeting. Our task-centred approach to family therapy means that we make numerous contracts, where co-therapy again brings clarity—we can see where the partner's explanations may be being misunderstood and, working "in tandem", we work on until we all have the same grasp of a point as far as possible. People seem to like workers who show they are clear in their purpose and able to communicate it clearly.

If we accept the comment in the introduction to this book that a family is like a labyrinth where the blind alleys are constantly changing, a partnership is very helpful to all concerned. In the face of such complexity we have the benefit of double observation and double feedback. This volume of information, however, has to lead to careful planning so that the pair share out the uses to be made of understandings of a situation and so they avoid tripping over each other in a session. This planning brings a great deal of structure into the work and we believe this structure is, in itself, helpful to chaotic family systems. If we allowed each other to be vague we would soon become confused. Structure brings its own support and we will show in Part II how this works out in planning for sessions with a particular family. We feel that the time spent is an indispensable requirement for fruitful sessions; it is as valuable as, and often takes longer than, the time actually spent with the family. Without a well worked out sharing of responsibilities, coupled with a flexible, responsive mutual support, it would be more difficult to puzzle one's way through the family maze, mapping the patterns of interaction, supporting and challenging family members as one goes along and all the while coping with a barrage of feeling. Shared responsibility means shared leadership but also stronger leadership where one therapist can relax and observe while the other leads, ready to counterpoint as the opportunity arises. Counterpointing is "backing each other up" in various ways. One picks up a point made by one's partner and focuses on it; one makes the same point as that made by the partner and stresses another aspect of it; one supports the other in a confrontation; one redirects the discussion while the other follows this diversion; one suggests some task or action in the session and the other gives a lead in promptly complying with the suggestion. An extension of this is where one therapist introduces the other as the "supervisor" for a particular session; the therapist "makes most of the going" while the supervisor comes in to counterpoint with the authority and expertness of a consultant. (In our work, however, we tend to present both of ourselves as experts, as already mentioned, since that is how we are usually introduced by the referring worker.)

Most of the literature on co-therapy mentions the use of structured roles within a session. Mueller *et al.* (1976),[5] for example, suggest that the male worker can identify with and support the males in the family, while being challenging towards the females, and the female worker can do the opposite. They say this structure brings "spontaneous support and confrontation" for each member of the family. It is difficult for one worker to maintain a balance between support and confrontation in a disorganised, yet rigid family and still prompt the system to change. Whilst we have tried this kind of role structuring on occasions, we use counterpointing much more. Skynner (1976)[6] supports the need for challenge as he discusses growth through challenge and intrusion of new information that disturbs the old (sick) stability and demands new coping skills. To so disturb severe cases may require the use of paradoxical injunctions or prescriptions and since these are rather tricky and need much careful thought, paired working is again a definite advantage. Planning ways to out-manoeuvre some dysfunctional family interactions and keeping these interactions, rather than the "sickness" of any individual, as the focus of the work is somehow less hazardous when one works with a partner. One can feel able to engage in a family discussion without the fear that one might get sucked into their whirlpool of fruitless, circular arguments, because one knows one's partner is a life-line who will spot this suction once it begins and stop it by changing direction. We will show an example of this later.

Co-therapy also has the benefit of providing the family with a model of a harmonious pair, showing a combination of spontaneity, attentiveness and responsiveness that mirrors good family relationships. The pair can be a model of reasonably negotiating partners who share authority, who communicate clearly, who can resolve disagreements, who can confirm and validate each other when in agreement, as well as being able to allow for and respect differences. It is vital to demonstrate to families how to validate each other. Skynner (1976)[7] adds that an opposite sex pair offers a "more adequate gender role model" which is especially valuable in cases where gender roles have been confusing or conflicting. The pair demonstrate parenting, shared authority and a control that sets an example for family members to control their behaviours.

Finally some thoughts on transference and projective identifications and counter transference. Because we enter the family's world as real people, as we have already described, the possibility of family members reacting to us as if we were significant people in their lives, on the basis of their transferred feelings, is reduced. We prefer this as our aim is to stick with the "here and now" of family problems, looking at and attempting to help family members to modify current interactional patterns. Similarly we do not encourage projective identifications. Dowling (1979)[8] describes these as a "commonly observed phenomenon in which the dysfunctional pattern of behaviour displayed by the family is unconsciously reproduced in the co-therapy relationship. It is important to stress the word "unconscious" because it is only when the therapists become aware of this that it becomes a therapeutic tool to share and work on with the family . . ." Some argue that this is a potent use of co-therapy. Walrond-Skinner (1976),[9] for instance, argues that "The most powerful and subtle use of co-therapy as a treatment technique is the use of the relationship to internalise the problems of the family group itself; to work them through and ultimately to resolve them during the course of the treatment step by step alongside the family." However, we do not try to further our therapeutic impact in this way. Instead we focus rigorously on changing the actual family transactions in the present and we actively encourage family members to work out their problems within the family, with each other, rather than within ourselves simultaneously. Our brief, time limited approach assists in this. Similarly the focus of our work and the fact that we work as a team also reduce the likelihood of counter-transferences developing, with all their complicating consequences.

All in all, therefore, we find working as a co-therapy pair has many advantages for our work with families. We are aware, however, that other family therapists prefer to work on their own (with back-up consultation and support) and that, indeed, the forms co-therapy may take vary (Dowling, 1979).[10] Perhaps the reader will need to experiment in order to discover what style of work suits him or her best and which families, with what problems, respond most easily to a co-therapy or uni-therapist approach.

This chapter concludes the theoretical discussion behind our practice. We see our practice as realistically based, drawing on the theory outlined in Part I. We hope to show in the case presentation which is to follow in Part II that once one gets the method right one does not need special charisma in order to get results! In presenting the Green family's case we will try to show that our method consists of co-therapy, using some of the concepts we have outlined to analyse problems and using a task-centred approach to tackle these problems. This involves making a detailed plan for each session, with a joint review after the sessions, leading to specific aims for future work.

References

1. Whitaker, C., A longitudinal view of therapy styles, in *Family Process*, **11**, 1 (1972).
2. Rice, D. G. *et al.*, Therapists' experience and styles as factors in co-therapy, in *Family Process*, **11**, 1 (1972).
3. Walrond-Skinner, S., Family Therapy: The Treatment of Natural Systems Lib. S/W, London, RKP (1976).
4. Mueller, P. S. *et al.*, A method of co-therapy for schizophrenic families, in *Family Process*, **15**, 2 (1976).
5. *Ibid.*
6. Skynner, R., *One Flesh: Separate Persons*, Constable (1976).
7. *Ibid.*
8. Dowling, E., Co-therapy: A clinical researcher's view, in Walrond-Skinner, S. (Ed.), *Family and Marital Psychotherapy*, RKP (1979).
9. Walrond-Skinner, S., *Op. Cit.* (1976).
10. Dowling, E., *Op. Cit.* (1979).

PART II

Applying Family Therapy—A Case Example

CHAPTER 5

The Green Family—Referral Information

In this chapter we will outline the information we were given about the Green family when we went to see the probation officer who was already working with them. Miss Scott was supervising Michael (aged 16) but she thought her work with him needed to be supplemented with efforts to modify family functioning as a whole. Not having the time to devote to this herself, she had requested our involvement.

As is usual when a family is referred to us we quickly noted down a family tree of the Greens. This immediately highlighted the fact that there were a number of fathers in this family and that, diagrammatically at least, Mr. Williams, Mrs. Green's cohabitee, was quite distanced from the children, with Mrs. Green acting as a kind of barrier. We wondered if actual family interactions would reflect this in any way?

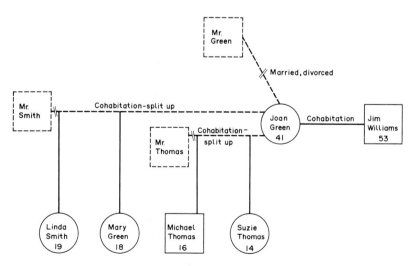

FIG. 5.1 A Family Tree

Miss Scott then gave us brief details of the family's history. Mrs. Green had married when she was eighteen-years-old. There were no children of the marriage and after the marriage broke up she had then cohabited with Mr. Smith. Mr. Smith had left her while she was pregnant with Mary. Then Mrs. Green had lived with Mr. Thomas for 10 years. This had been, apparently, a difficult relationship—Mr. Thomas had battered his wife and he had, we were told, been a heavy drinker. Mrs. Green had left him when Michael was about 6 years old and had gone, with the children, to live with her mother before being re-housed. Mrs. Green had obtained her divorce 6 years previously. Mrs. Green had known Mr. Williams before she had split up with Mr. Thomas but she and the children had only finally moved in to live in Mr. William's home $2\frac{1}{2}$ years ago.

One interesting point that Miss Scott mentioned was that Mrs. Green was not very keen to discuss her marital status or history—it made her feel "got at", as did the fact of her children's illegitimacy. She argued that such matters were not relevant to the current problems. Obviously delving into old history would make Mrs. Green feel threatened and put her on the defensive—given our preference for sticking with the "here and now" we felt she might be able to relax a bit, and stay "engaged" with our efforts to improve family functioning.

The current problems centred round Michael and Miss Scott reported that recently the family had been seriously requesting his removal because of the endless arguments and confrontations. Apparently things had calmed down a little since then, with people reporting that Michael could behave reasonably well when on his own with either Mrs. Green or Mr. Williams but that trouble started if the three of them were at home together and when Michael was with his sisters.

Miss Scott described Michael as an overweight, lethargic young man (though he used to be quite sporty). She felt he was immature, selfish, unsociable and surly. He had truanted in the last year of school (spending a great deal of time with a nineteen-year-old girl) and he had been a problem at school because of his bullying and uncooperative behaviour. He had only recently started work and was apparently reluctant to pay his board and lodging at home. He had few friends and interests and Miss Scott thought he spent most of his time watching TV. Michael had appeared in court once, about 6 months previously. He had admitted offences of theft and robbery. Another lad had been involved who had been in trouble with the courts before. Apparently one of the offences had been rather nasty involving the bullying of another boy and the magistrates had threatened Michael with detention centre. However, this had been partly averted by Mr. Williams attending court and speaking up for him and in the end he had been fined, ordered to attend attendance centre for 24 hours and had been placed on supervision. Since then Michael had reported to Miss Scott very regularly and had been to the attendance centre. When pushed really hard, Miss Scott said, he did seem to respond to advice and guidance though he was often not very forthcoming in their meetings. Michael apparently blamed Mr. Williams for the break-up of the relationship between his mother and father and this often came up in rows at home, with Michael suggesting he had some damaging "dope" on his step-father. Michael seemed to be jealous of his sisters and argued that they got more attention and things from his parents than he did. Mrs. Green argued that if anything it was the other way round. Certainly though Michael picked fights with his sisters.

We learnt a little about the girls. Linda was reported to be ESN, a pleasant, sensitive girl (somewhat outside of the disharmony) who worked regularly and attended literacy classes. Mary and Suzie, however, did their share of provoking and could really upset Michael by calling him a "bastard". Mary worked and Suzie was at school.

The family lived in a modern three-bedroom terraced house, with a through lounge-cum-dining room. We wondered whether this meant the family was rather cramped, with 2 adults and 4 adolescent aged children. Mrs. Green worked as a waitress every weekday evening (from 5–8.15 pm.) and Mr. Williams worked shifts as a security man—usually at nights. His job was well paid and in fact he only worked about 3 nights a week. (All this meant, of course, that we were going to have to put ourselves out as regards visiting so the whole family could be available.)

The only other information we found out about any of the family members concerned Mr. Thomas. He was disabled in some way and was living with a married daughter. Michael maintained that Mr. Thomas was the only person who cared for him but, even so, Michael only visited him infrequently and irregularly. At the beginning of the new year (about 6 weeks previously) Michael had left home and gone to stay with the married daughter (his sister or half-sister?) for the weekend. However, she had not been able to put up with him.

Obviously this information was both sketchy and not necessarily entirely accurate. One can imagine that one could spend many "happy" hours with the family trying to sort out their family history and teasing out new details but as the reader will probably notice we did not seek elaboration of a great deal of what we were told at the referral meeting because we were much more interested in how people were getting on with each other currently, because understanding current dynamics would give us clues about how to intervene.

We learnt from Miss Scott that she had told the family about our existence and about our interest in family therapy. She had explained that both Michael and his family were free to pull out of the sessions with us at any time but she had strongly recommended them to give us a try. The family had apparently thought that Michael would not be willing to participate but in discussion with him separately Miss Scott had thought he was very curious about what we would be trying to do. She had pointed out to him that as we would be discussing him in the family sessions it was in his best interests to be there to put his point of view. The family had, therefore, agreed to meet us and were expecting us to make contact.

Finally then we agreed the following with Miss Scott:

1. We would go ahead to fix a first visit to the family. (They were on the telephone and Miss Scott said that making contact this way would be fine.)
2. We would be negotiating a contract with the family to have approximately 4 exploratory sessions of $1-1\frac{1}{2}$ hours with the whole and/or parts of the family for a beginning before deciding on any further aims and methods of work.
3. We would send Miss Scott brief, written summaries of our work with the family.
4. Miss Scott would be continuing to see Michael weekly for reporting and she would let us know if there was anything important that we needed to be aware of.

So, then, it was up to us to plan our first visit to the family and to fix a time when we could meet them all together for a first session.

CHAPTER 6

The First Session—Initial Visit to the Family

We telephoned the family to say we had met Miss Scott and that we understood they were expecting us to contact them about arranging a visit to their home. Mrs. Green answered the call and made a comment that she would try anything to improve matters. Through her it was arranged that we would visit at 8.15 p.m., a convenient time for the whole family. She promised to make sure the whole family would be there.

Perhaps we should make it clear here that if we could have all got together during working hours we would have preferred this to having to make late evening visits. However, our own work commitments and those of the family members usually prohibited this. We are not suggesting that family therapy can only be done at night! What we are suggesting is that one needs to be reasonably flexible in order to be able to meet up with all the family members involved in a dysfunctional family system. We also do not feel it is essential to always meet families in their own homes. Important observations can be made during such visits but there may be good reasons for inviting families to office-based sessions. For example, a family's motivation to work for change may be tested by this means or it may have proved impossible to create a reasonably uninterrupted setting within the home in which to conduct the business of the session. However, in our case we did not have a suitable office to which to invite the Green family, nor did home visits create great problems.

To return to our discussion of making contact with the Green family, after arranging a visit, we met to clarify our aims for the first session, and to work out a plan to achieve these. The aims were typical of most first meetings with a family. We wanted to make contact with them as people, to agree a contract for some more exploratory sessions, to begin to explore the problems and to engage them as a family in beginning to work on the problems by setting them an exploratory task. Set out below then is the plan we arrived at, showing which of us would be responsible for leading in each intervention:

Session 1	Responsibility of	
Content	PO'B	HM
1. Introductions—ourselves and the family.	PO'B to observe interactions, to support Mr. W. if necessary (e.g. sit next to him)	✓
2. Explanation of our role, our work and our relationship with Miss Scott. Our understanding of their situation gleaned from her.		✓
3. Negotiate a contract for 3/4 exploratory sessions with the whole or parts of the family.		✓
4. Establish ground rules for sessions: include— a. people have different perspectives on things so everyone needs a say, b. everyone should feel free to disagree, with us too, c. there should be no recriminations after sessions, d. confidentiality exists between our-selves, the family and Miss Scott.		✓
5. Invite the family to tell us about their difficulties (adding a warning that we have no magic—they know their family best and have to take charge of changes.)	✓	HM to focus on getting details, seeking clarification, engaging everyone and supporting Michael and Mrs. Green if necessary.
	Both to act as models of constructive, effective communication.	
6. Arrange next session, decide on with whom. Set the family the task of completing the questionnaire we'd devised.	✓	✓

The plan indicates that, after introductions, we would carefully explain who we were, our backgrounds and present work. We would give a summary of what Miss Scott had told us about their difficulties. In doing this we would give our full names and hope to get on first name terms with them eventually. We prefer to get on first name terms with people to encourage a more informal, open atmosphere. Moreover, when we work as a pair we call each other by our christian names in the sessions and we would not want family members to feel that they still had to address us by our surnames, which might create an unnecessary distance between us and them. We recognise, however, that workers have differing views on the use of first names with clients. Clearly this is something that has to be discussed within the co-therapy team so that a clear message is given to the family about what "rules" (if any) apply in this area.

Before proceeding further, we would attempt to get their agreement to further sessions which would be followed by an evaluation with them, as a result of which we would work out agreements for further work if necessary. Next we proposed to establish the four ground rules noted in the plan, before inviting them to talk about their problems. We thought we would emphasise that we had no magical ways of changing them and that in discussing change we would be merely pointing out certain choices. They were the people who would be deciding what to do. This would help to avoid creating resistance since it implies the paradox that they would have to change spontaneously. HM would lead the interviewing, PO'B would come in to clarify particular items if necessary but his main jobs would be observing and offering support to Mr. Williams if needed. We thought he might be the member who was under pressure or being excluded, being a nominal step-father to four teenagers, rejected by Michael and the fourth man in Mrs. Green's life. HM would attempt to sit near Michal and be supportive to him since he might be under pressure as the "cause of the troubles". She would also try to support Mrs. Green if necessary. We planned to end the session by summing up and leaving them with some homework—an exploratory task. They would each be asked to think about the family and complete the questionnaire we would leave with them before the next visit (the date of which we would then fix). A copy of the questionnaire we drew up is set out below:

1. Can you finish this sentence:
   "I think the biggest problem our family has is ....
   ....
   ....

2. If possible could you explain the problem in these ways:
   What actually happens?

   Who does it affect?

   How does it affect them?

   Where does it happen?

   When does it happen?

   Why do *you* think it happens?

   How do you think it could be tackled?

3. Now, can you finish this sentence:

"I think we also have problems with ....

....

....

4. And this sentence:
   "What I *like* about our family is ....

....

....

5. And finally, try and find one word that describes yourself and each
   member of your family:
   Name   *1 word to describe them*

We hoped to move the session along fairly briskly, reckoning to finish after about an hour and certainly aiming to take not more than $1\frac{1}{2}$ hours. (Otherwise the session would become tiring for us and them probably and hence less productive.) Afterwards one of us would write up the process of the session as fully as possible and the other would prepare notes on the individual family members, plus assessment notes on the family's problems. Later on we would meet to review the session and to decide what needed to be done next.

In this presentation (in this and subsequent chapters) we will combine both sets of notes to make up a full account of the process of work. This will appear on the left hand sides of the pages; on the right we will make comments and note links with the theory and ideas from the literature outlined in Part I of the book.

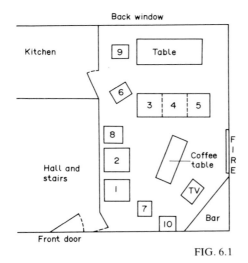

Seats 1–5 = three piece suite

Seats 6–10 = dining chairs

(In this three bedroom house Michael and Mary shared one bedroom.)

(Jim lived here alone until the others moved in. It is a modern council house with good material standards.)

FIG. 6.1

First, however, we give a sketch of the living room (Fig. 6.1) and brief pen pictures of the family members as we found them in the first session.

Pen pictures of family members

Joan Green —a short, dumpy lady with mousy-coloured, shortish curly hair. Quite large eyes, a bright smile, talkative, quite forceful. Still in her working clothes—a smock.

Jim Williams—medium height, a bit of a tummy on him but otherwise slim. Short, straight black hair—thinning but not bald. Ruddy, weathered complexion. Quieter spoken than Joan but not afraid to have his say.

Linda —slightly mongoloid in appearance. Shy and a little giggly but did contribute though it was not easy to hear her as she put her hand over her mouth a lot. Mousy, short hair, pleasantly dressed.

Mary —fair complexion, blonde medium length hair. Wearing a blue overall. Very outspoken and quite noisy but was good-humoured too. Perched on the edge of her seat to make sure she was involved.

Michael Overweight, solid looking. Darker hair than his mother, Linda and Mary. Kept his hand over his mouth a good deal— behind his hand he was often smiling mischievously while, at the same time, he tried to look sullen and defiant (at which he sometimes succeeded).

Suzie —Slim, dark haired. Easy to tell she and Michael were full brother and sister. Bouncy, chatty with a bright smile. Full of confidence. Nicely dressed.

We arrived promptly, to be welcomed by Jim and shown into the living room. All the family was there. The TV was on but was quickly turned off by Joan, with a small protest from Michael, though Joan countered that he didn't know anything about the politics being discussed on the programme anyway. Linda was in seat 1, Michael in seat 3 and Mary in seat 5. Suzie was poring over her homework in seat 9. For a moment we thought she wasn't going to join us but she soon did. Both she and Mary were unsmiling when we arrived but once introduced they relaxed, smiling happily and becoming thoroughly involved.

Comments

When invited to sit down HM sat in seat 4, between Michael and Mary. Joan sat in seat 2 and Suzie moved to seat 8. This left seat 7 for PO'B.

This helps HM to support Michael more easily.
It is best that workers do not sit together. It is easier to communicate when not side by side and the family may feel less threatened if not "up against" an impenetrable pair, seeking to exclude the family.

It was hard for HM to see Jim who, positioned on seat 6, seemed to be rather "out of it" though he in fact participated well enough.

Suzie is seated between Joan and Jim. Does she come between them relationship-wise? A possible hypothesis but not, obviously, for sharing with the family. As Haley comments, such interpretations are not helpful to families.

We began by introducing ourselves and the family was introduced by Joan. We explained our interest in family work and our other roles. Joan quickly pointed out that Mary was pregnant and marrying in a few months' time. She would be leaving to live with her husband's mother. As if trying to relate to us, Joan asked if HM (as a former social worker) could help Mary get a house. HM muttered about Mary visiting the housing department and getting on the list and so that matter was dropped. (It was also suggested that Miss Scott might be approached.)

The "social stage" of the session.

Someone leaving the system. A developmental stage that often brings problems.

HM deliberately took a low-key line on this, not wishing to get side-tracked into this.

We explained that Miss Scott had told us something of their difficulties and that we understood that when the family was all together the sparks flew etc. Joan, who was the spokesman at this stage, agreed that it was Michael who got them all going.

Keep this kind of introductory remark fairly vague so as not to channel their responses. Focus on the family aspect of the problem.

At this point we made an agreement with them to hold 3 or 4 exploratory sessions with parts or the whole of the family and we established the ground rules set out in our plan. We said *we* thought such ground rules were helpful and they readily accepted them.

Initial contract made to examine their situation.

HM then asked the family to describe the difficulties they were having. Joan, Mary and Suzie were quite vocal, talking vaguely about rows going on about all sorts of things, Michael wanting his own way and being jealous of his sisters because he felt that he got less attention than they did. He apparently also resented their use of "a certain word". Early on Mary and Suzie admitted to being able to provoke Michael. There was a tense moment when PO'B asked Michael what the "certain word" was, with which his sisters so easily upset him. Michael coloured deeply and refused to say the word—it was Jim who said it was "bastard". He and Joan said they didn't hear the girls using it, Michael maintained it was a regular feature of rows. Joan and the girls agreed that the latter did not mind being illegitimate—it was Michael who really was upset by it. (It seemed that Linda steered clear of the tensions by retreating upstairs to her room or going out with her fiancé.) Michael had hit Mary and had "gone for" Joan. Jim was obviously angry with him and suggested that he himself could become violent towards Michael—"if it goes on he will see the other side of me". Meanwhile Suzie was helping to describe Michael's violence—in general the girls played down the provocation they were responsible for.

The "problem exploration" stage.

Examples of behaviour that enables "the problem" to persist.

We asked the family to tell us about a particular incident in more detail. We soon heard of the matter of who decided what programmes on TV were to be viewed. What emerged was that it seemed that when Michael was on his own with Linda she opted out of the battle and didn't push her choice. Mary often went out anyway, after seeing "Coronation Street". Jim and Michael often agreed about

Seeking specificity and, hopefully, an example of their negative circular interaction.

what to watch and Joan said she got her own way. Suzie squabbled a lot with Michael over TV viewing. However, when Michael was on his own with the three girls he insisted on getting his own way, resorting to physical violence if necessary. PO'B pressed Michael quite hard on the unreasonableness of this but he maintained he wouldn't give an inch, that he should be able to view what he wanted. HM asked him to imagine how he would feel if he magnanimously allowed others their programme choices. He said he would feel bad and would not do it. PO'B pointed out that his approach was not realistic—at work, for instance, if he tried to get his own way all the time he would quickly be isolated. He seemed to shrug his shoulders and stood his ground.

Michael emerging as a "parental child"?

This pressing brings out how serious the matter is but it must not go too far. Better to go with the system—we could say that Michael couldn't be that unreasonable for nothing—it must be serving some purpose and be maintained by others' behaviour.

Later, Suzie described what often happens between herself and Michael over the TV. She might ask him if she might switch channels. He would say "No" but a couple of minutes later he would tell her she could switch over. She would then tell him to do it himself—he had legs—and so it would develop into a squabble!

Circularity! He cannot win. Suzie is as much a "cause" of the trouble as Michael is.

This led on to a discussion about the fact that Michael seemed to feel that he received less attention than his sisters, both from Joan and from Jim, whom he constantly referred to as his mother's "fancy man". Jim, who had been in and out of the kitchen making coffee, talked very seriously about loving them as if they were his own. Suzie said she was spoilt by Jim—Mary loudly agreed, saying she'd been "ruined" by him. Jim said he showed his affection for them all but in different ways because they were all individuals and he maintained that Michael was wrong to think that he did not care about him too. There was

Michael seeks to exclude Jim, who is functioning in a kind of butler role, treating the family still as guests in his home.

Jim has a particular liking for Suzie. Is this creating problems between Jim and Joan? Is Michael being scapegoated as a result (to take the focus off such trouble)? Another possible hypothesis . . .

a touching moment, which caused Michael some embarrassment, when all the family expressed affection for him, with Mary reporting that she had wept when she had mistakenly thought that he had been sent to detention centre.

Then we got an account of how "jumpy" Michael could be. They teased him about how frightened he had been recently when he had heard footsteps upstairs and had thought he had been alone in the house. It had, in fact, been Linda. Joan went on to tell us about his fears about ghosts but we did not take the matter up.

Returning to Michael's jealousy, Joan said that he could not appreciate the difference between the love one had for one's children and the love one had for one's partner. HM felt she was suggesting that he thought she had a fixed amount of love and that if she gave some to Jim, this meant less for Michael. Michael staunchly maintained that she should put her children before Jim. Joan thought that if she favoured any of her children it was Linda because of her backwardness. Joan thought that she and Jim tried to give the children all they wanted, that they encouraged democratic living and that their own parents had been much tougher than they ever were. Joan talked about rowing with Jim over Michael—she said she probably backed Michael up more than she should. Jim apparently complained about the soft line taken with "villains"—he said he had been through a lot himself but that he would only enforce his own will if things could not be worked out in any other way.

Comments

Fairly typical of the contradictions found in families and evidence for us that there is something positive going for this family.

Such a topic is too convenient as a red herring! Though perhaps it was evidence that perhaps Michael wasn't so tough after all. (Similar tales came up in later sessions—we ignored them by and large.)

Another triangular relationship? Or at least some cross-generational alliance?

And there is some split in the "parental pair".

Comments

Joan complained that Michael did not respect her, that he abused her verbally at times. She thought his father encouraged him to behave badly towards her—i.e. he called her a slut etc. Later she said that all the tensions at home were really getting to her. When she and Jim were out at work they were on tenterhooks about how things would be when they got home. She added that she was having medical treatment for high blood pressure and was attending hospital for check-ups.

This admission that she was being seriously affected, helps in engaging her—*she* has problems in coping, for whatever reason, including Michael's misbehaviour.

We discussed Michael's lack of friends. The three girls had boyfriends. Michael fought with them too, except Mary's who was a karate expert! Jim wished Michael had a girlfriend, Michael reckoned he had thousands! Jim and Joan thought he had only had the nineteen-year-old whom they had disapproved of. Michael said he had had more, while Suzie said he had had more than one. Michael defended himself by suggesting that what was the point of having girlfriends if no one in the family ever liked them anyway? The general consensus was that it was not surprising Michael had few friends—he didn't make himself very likeable. HM suggested that people could not offer much love if they did not get anything in return. Michael didn't respond to this.

Evidence that Michael responds to what he sees as a superior force?! Does this give hope for the future if the parental coalition can be strengthened?

There was next a brief diversion—Mary's expected baby was discussed. Michael hoped it would be a boy—we joked that perhaps he felt surrounded by females!

And that Jim was not much of an ally?

We asked about the other ways in which the family organised itself. It became apparent that Jim and Joan did most things around the house and only expected the children to keep their own rooms tidy.

How domestic chores are managed says a lot about family roles and relationships. In this family the parental pair seem to be doing too much, not delegating sufficient responsibility to the teenagers—generally treating them like youngsters while expecting maturity from them in relationships.

Michael loudly proclaimed that he was the one who kept his and Mary's room tidy and that she was very untidy. She and the family agreed, though she said the room was mostly full of Michael's stuff anyway.

The overcrowding in this household must be contributing to the tension. Mary's departure may ease things somewhat.

Jim seemed to run a hotel service as regards preparing food for people as and when they came in. Mary and Linda paid Joan £7 a week board. Michael paid her £8, the extra pound covering his lunches, which Mary and Linda got free at work. Michael resented having to pay the extra—he said that was not his fault that there were no free meals at his work. All in all, Jim and Joan reckoned the children had an easy time of things. At least twice they commented that materially the family was better off then ever before (Jim had given them a nice home) and there was no need for them to be so unhappy. There seemed to be real regret that people could not be on better terms with each other. Most of the blame was again laid at Michael's door. He was described as "selfish" more than once and Suzie said he was a "split personality" who would not change. Michael sat grimly through this. A good deal of shouting went on. PO'B pointed out to them how loudly and harshly they spoke to each other. He said that it would be necessary to calm things down a bit. Suzie said that Michael would not mean it even if he promised to change!

We wondered about the fairness of this as Michael earned the least.

This typifies how Michael was being labelled (and scapegoated?) in the family.

The suggestion that they all were harsh helped to widen the issue and undermine their usual labelling.

Again, he cannot win!

We began to wind up the session at this point by suggesting that perhaps we could make some suggestions about how they might behave a bit differently towards each other. Here Joan jumped in fairly stubbornly, saying she didn't see why she should change any more. PO'B suggested that if it helped the family in the long run (to make life more

Comments

pleasant) wasn't it worth it? We suggested to Michael that if he was not prepared to change a little in return for the other five members changing a little this would be short-sighted. He did not reply.

While keeping some focus on Michael (thereby going with the family and not seeking to change their definition of the problem) we were still implying that the others should change first.

We proceeded to explain the task we were wanting them to do—i.e. to complete the questionnaires we had brought, before the next session. They became intrigued. We explained that they should state their own views but they could discuss with others. We made special arrangements for Linda—someone would help her fill her's in. They all seemed amenable to the idea though Michael muttered about not bothering to fill his in. When, however, strangely, Jim began to collect the papers together (which HM had distributed to all six family members) Michael refused to part with his copy. When HM gently "twisted his arm" to fill it in he grinned happily enough. (Much of the time he had a twinkle in his eye that suggested he was, in part, enjoying his role.)

This led us to wonder whether the others weren't making the mistake of taking Michael too seriously.

The final few minutes were spent very informally. The family was impressed and flattered that we had come to see them in our spare time, PO'B even having sacrificed a badminton game! "And you are lecturers too"!!, commented Jim. They asked again about our training etc. Joan had seen a "Man Alive" programme on family therapy but had thought that such things were just fiction. We discussed again our interest in families and our experiences of working with them. Jim said he had not believed in seeking outside help for their family problems in the past but now he was willing to try anything.

It was important for them to know a good deal about us, not only as workers but also as people. They were sharing personal issues with us and they needed to experience the *persons* behind the therapist roles.

Comments

After some negotiating we settled that the next session would be with the whole family at 8.15 pm. on March 6th. We mentioned the possibility of seeing parts of the family group in later sessions. As we left, $1\frac{1}{2}$ hours had passed.

In evaluating the session immediately afterwards, we considered that we had followed the plan and had achieved our aims. We had experienced a good deal of warmth in the family, which seemed a hopeful sign, and we had engaged with them in a positive way.

CHAPTER 7

The Second Session—Exploring the Family's Difficulties

We came away from our first session with the Green family with a number of initial impressions and tentative hypotheses about their functioning and problems. Below, in list form, is a summary of them:

1. In spite of everything, we felt that there was a lot of warmth and positive feeling between family members. The evidence for this included:
   —the fairly relaxed, agreeable way in which everyone joined in the session,
   —the general expressions of affection for Michael as Mary described her upset when she thought that he'd been sent to detention centre,
   —Jim's public declaration of his love for all his step-children,
   —the feeling of regret that was expressed by Joan and Jim that although materially better off than ever before they couldn't live together more harmoniously as a family.

2. *However*, it seemed that the family members kept getting into unproductive squabbles (dysfunctional sequences of behaviour) over various aspects of household organisation and management. Deciding on TV viewing seemed to be one especially fraught area. Particularly worrying was the amount of *physical* violence that was being reported.

3. Joan's health was suffering as a result of the difficulties—she needed relief in both psychological and practical terms.

4. As part of the dysfunctional sequences of behaviour, Michael's behaviour was often being labelled in very negative terms. Certainly he was behaving in an aggressive, stubborn and uncompromising way but was he being pushed into this role, partly because people were taking him far too seriously? So often during the interview with the Green family we thought we could detect a twinkle in his eye and a mischievous grin behind the hand held over his mouth.

5. We noticed that Jim seemed to be very much on the periphery at times. He seemed to be functioning as a butler in his own home—ushering people in and out, making refreshments, sitting on a hard chair on the edge of the family group. How far had his step-relative position in the family been worked out to the satisfaction and comfort of all concerned?

6. This led us on to wonder about the relationship between Jim and Joan. Neither of us came away from the first session with a clear impression of the strength or otherwise of their relationship. How far had they worked out their "marital" and "parental" functioning? What sort of coalitions were they presenting to the rest of the family? We noted that there was evidence that Michael was trying to act as a parental child, bossing his sisters around and that a special closeness seemed to exist between Jim and Suzie.

Therefore we hypothesised that:

7. In this family Jim and Joan's marital and parental functioning was problematic (probably because of failures in the negotiation of the normal tasks associated with the creation of a family with step-relatives, complicated by the fact that in this family adjustments were needed anyway in order to accommodate the changing needs of the adolescent aged children [stages 4 and 5 of the Carter and McGoldrick family life cycle.]) As a result the children had been "allowed" to cross generational boundaries and to get in between Joan and Jim, further increasing their pain. Thus Suzie was "intruding" in their love relationship and Michael was trying to move in on their parental responsibilities.

8. We also thought, however, that these marital and parental difficulties were not perhaps recognised, let alone aired. We wondered if there was an element of scapegoating going on in that Michael was being presented as the problem. Perhaps his behaviour was being negatively labelled and encouraged in order to take the focus of the pain and discomfort in Joan and Jim's relationship?

All these points then were discussed when we met to plan our second session with the family. We were pleased that we had arranged another whole family interview at this stage as we realised we needed to explore our first impressions and hypotheses (points 7 and 8) more fully. However, we were already thinking in terms of possible tasks and strategies that might ease the family's situation:

e.g. seeing Joan and Jim on their own to re-affirm and strengthen their functioning,

seeing the children separately to emphasise their generational "place" in the family and to work out with them ways of relieving the burden on Joan and Jim as regards household tasks, in the cause of improving Joan's health,

asking family members to sit in certain chairs in the family session so that the generational boundary was clarified,

interfering with the unproductive squabbling and Michael's attempts to parent his sisters by suggesting "absurd" and perhaps paradoxical tasks (for instance, getting Michael and his sisters to role play a row for us; suggesting Michael try to provoke his sisters; putting Michael in charge of the family's TV viewing.)

Therefore we had all sorts of possibilities before us, as well as the fact that we needed to discuss the contents of the questionnaires family members had been asked to complete before session 2. In the end then we settled on this plan for our next family session:

Session 2	Responsibility of	
Content	PO'B	HM
1. Manoeuvre seating arrangements with a view to getting Jim and Joan sitting together and Michael and Mary together.		✔
2. Ask for completed questionnaires. Share their contents, summarise points made.		✔
3. Initiate family sculpts and drawings.	✔	
4. Summarise what has been learnt so far—the base line.	✔	✔
5. Negotiate the next two sessions— (a) with Jim and Joan (b) with the children.	✔	✔
6. Suggest a further task—in relation to the management of the family's TV viewing, (say 5 days of Michael in charge and 5 days of the girls in charge), ↓ demonstrate the use of a cushion to improve communications, ↓ nominate a monitor ↓ no violence rule.	✔ ✔	✔

The therapeutic aims behind manoeuvring the seating arrangements were three: firstly we wanted to highlight Jim's and Joan's coalition, secondly we wanted to make it harder for Michael and Mary to row (it *is* a lot more difficult to conduct a row with someone when you're sitting next to them), and thirdly we saw it as a way of establishing ourselves as people who would suggest changes and as a way of setting the scene for sculpting (which would involve people in moving about). Discussing the contents of the questionnaires (*if* the family had completed this task) and undertaking family sculpts and drawings would provide more evidence for or against our first impressions and hypotheses. Our aim in suggesting the TV viewing management exercise was to reframe the situation (by giving Michael legitimate authority to manage the family's viewing) and, paradoxically, to suggest that the family stop trying to oppose his bossiness but to go along with it. We would introduce the whole exercise as a continuation of the exploratory process and we would ask someone to monitor which arrangement (Michael in charge or the girls in charge) produced most rows. (Secretly, of course, we hoped they would thwart our efforts by rowing less!) Finally setting up separate sessions with Joan and Jim and with the children for our next two sessions followed directly from our hypotheses about the nature of the family's difficulties. The mere fact of seeing them separately would help to highlight the need for generational differences, the need for there to be space between sub-systems. (And, of course, this was in keeping with a systems approach to family therapy in that we were choosing to work with parts of the whole system knowing that change in one part would have reverberations throughout the whole system.)

There was a "hiccup" in the arrangements for meeting with the family for the second time. Joan Green rang Miss Scott to postpone the meeting because she had to go out with Mary to sort out some wedding details. She reported that she had enjoyed the first session and wanted to be there for the second. We rang the family back (and made sure they had our telephone numbers so they could contact us directly in future) and arranged to visit instead on March 10th, at 8.15 pm. again. Jim Williams who took the call was quite formal in his manner over the telephone, calling PO'B "Sir". At the time we were mildly alarmed at this postponement but eventually we concluded that really we only needed the family to be "*sufficiently*" rather than "*optimally*" motivated!

	Comments
On arrival we were met by Jim. In the living room (see Figure 6.1), Suzie was in seat 9 doing her homework, Mary was in seat 5 and Joan was in seat 2. Linda was in seat 1. PO'B sat in seat 7 but HM hesitated about taking seat 4 (as planned) and suggested that Mary go to 4 because HM could see everyone more easily from seat 5. Mary moved as requested. HM hoped that this would leave seat 3 vacant for Michael when he arrived but as soon as Mary moved Linda got up and moved from seat 1 into seat 3! (Mary was in her dressing gown—not feeling well—acidic stomach associated with pregnancy.)	We made no comment about this—but wondered whether if the worker gets one member of a family to make even minor symbolic changes this leads to other people making moves/ changes?
Seat 8 was missing and seat 6 was behind the settee (3, 4 and 5.) When Jim finally sat down he went to seat 6. HM indicated that it was hard to see him without much turning round and so he moved his chair round next to 3.	More evidence of him being on the "edge" of things?

Comments

Suzie at first hesitated about joining us and leaving her homework but she agreed to join us when everyone asked her. She sat on the arm of chair 2, between Jim and Joan.

Suzie getting in between them again?

When we arrived Michael was upstairs and he was very slow to come down. Jim went twice to call him and said he was being "funny". We asked "how?" and Jim said "He says he didn't know you had come". Jim made coffee while we were waiting for Michael.

Michael's hesitation is probably quite understandable—he'll feel under some threat as the focus of work.

More evidence of Jim's butler role—this and taking responsibility for calling Michael.

As Jim arrived with the coffee he told us that he had lost all the forms we had left last time, including Mary's which she'd completed—he'd thrown them out with some papers. He was very apologetic. We made no comment on this other than to make some vague sound expressing disappointment and we said that we would have to carry on without them.

How had this happened? Was it a genuine accident? (We'd been puzzled by Jim's attempts to collect them up at the end of the last session.) There were all sorts of possibilities but we feel it is unproductive to go into a long inquest on such matters usually. We prefer to keep things moving. So we just express regret and carry on. In a sense, having "let us down" the family might feel more obliged to go along with our next suggestion!

Then Michael joined us. (PO'B could hear him lingering in the hallway before he entered the room.) He reported that he had not completed his form, he said he couldn't understand the questions. He sat in seat 1.

HM didn't then ask him and Mary to relocate themselves next to each other. She felt that this might immediately set up a confrontation with Michael.

Before moving on PO/B summed up where we got to last time, keeping the focus on the "problem"—Michael was difficult and violent and it seemed the family as a whole could not get on with him, especially when they were in a large group together. They were all unhappy and had agreed to work with us for a while, to try and help them overcome the problem. This would involve them in making changes, even though they were not person-

This wasn't in the plan but as, with one thing and another, the session had got off to a ragged start, it did have the useful effect of "calling the meeting to order" as well as providing continuity between sessions and a chance for family members to raise anything immediately on their minds.

ally at fault. There was some element of provocation involved. Mother was suffering from high blood pressure and so they would "give it a try", "try to start afresh".

PO'B moved on to what was presented as an alternative to the missing forms, to round off our understanding of the problem. He had brought some sheets of paper and felt-tip pens and suggested we could look at the situation in another way—by showing on paper how they were towards each other. He drew a J. for Joan and said "if that's Mum, where are the others?" Suzie quickly took this up and said "You mean how near to her are we?" She moved to the coffee table with PO'B and the others moved forward on their seats to watch. Suzie completed Figure 1 (see next page) and we discussed it. She put herself between Joan and Jim, closer to Joan than the others, with Michael furthest away. PO'B asked if Joan would agree and she said that even though Linda used to be very near, due to her "slowness", she was now growing away—courting—whereas Suzie was still at school. PO'B thought that Linda was not too happy about this.

The others were asked to do similar drawings and each was discussed. Mary did Figure 2, Michael Figure 3, Joan Figure 4, Jim Figure 5 and finally Linda Figure 6. Each was briefly discussed (highlighting their similar and different features.) Michael's drawing showed himself higher up on the paper and we asked if this meant anything. He agreed with someone's suggestion that he was a "big-head". Throughout the exercise it was necessary to keep reminding them that this should show how things *were* and gradually there was less tale-telling about past or present rows. (We were not interested in seeking reasons *why*

Comments

However, although accepting the presenting problem, the effect on the family as a whole was stressed.

Suzie proved to be very useful in terms of picking up the suggestions we made—now and later in the sculpts.

(Or indeed about much of the session. Later on she showed considerable anger.)

All the drawings we felt showed quite a family muddle—with Michael out in the cold each time, and Joan and Jim mixed up (and not always together) in the children's group. (Joan's drawing put Jim and Suzie together very clearly.) Further evidence we felt for our hypotheses.

As we've already indicated we focus on the "here and now". What could a discussion of past events tell us? We felt there was enough evidence that this group of people saw themselves as a family (in Pollak's terms), that they wanted things to be better between them

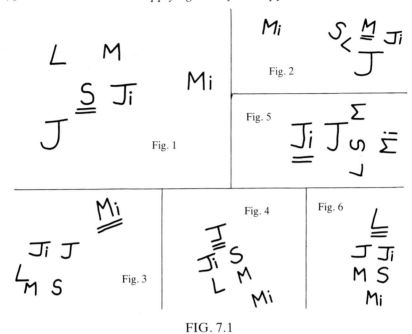

FIG. 7.1

things were like they were, but merely in obtaining a description of current interactions.)

We began to ask if these drawings really showed how it was with the family, which led on to our suggesting that 2-dimensional drawings were limiting. So we suggested a sculpt or tableau. When this was further explained Suzie again jumped into the centre. She stood Joan and the three girls in a line facing Michael, with their hands up to save their faces and with Joan's hands on Michael's chest, as if to hold him back. All the women were to look scared. Jim was placed by Suzie at the end of the line pointing at Michael. Michael was instructed to put his fists up, looking threatening. The sculpt complete,

Comments

now. If current interactions are being directly affected by something in the past it will emerge in discussions of those current interactions. *Then* it may be relevant to discuss the past.

At this point we moved the coffee table to make a space. Taking this initiative helps to get the family into action. Be confident and energetic.

we asked them to hold still a minute and to think about how it felt. Then we sat down and reviewed the sculpt. Michael said it wasn't "too bad". PO'B suggested "not too good either?" and Michael agreed—he wasn't exactly happy with all the others against him. Joan was next asked how it felt and she hesitated (distrustingly?). PO'B said that he was not asking out of curiosity but so that the others would understand. She then said it was a bit unfair and hard to say—she had asked herself why she stayed with them all— she could have left them all "in care". "But you were not that kind of mum who could do that" it was suggested and she was nearly in tears. Some of the others, Suzie and Michael we think, indicated how good it was to hear her say that. They told us Mum had left once—Jim had followed her round the block and had brought her back. The others all said the sculpt felt terrible, especially Jim. Linda expressed a lot of anger against Michael, saying he should be locked up. PO'B strongly disagreed.

At this stage PO'B was thinking "should we get some others to sculpt as this was only Suzie's impression?" HM, however, suggested that someone sculpt how they would like the family to be and this proved the right move and very productive. We focused on Michael who felt he could draw how the family should be. He completed this (Figure 7.2 overleaf), showing everyone smiling with himself sideways and large.

We questioned the various placings and he said that it wasn't right, so PO'B moved the coffee table again and invited Michael to use people again and show it better! He sculpted the family standing close together, in a circle, Joan next to Jim, Jim next to Mary, Mary

Comments

It is important to "freeze" a sculpt for a moment and to get people to think about how it feels. And, of course, the feedback after a sculpt is crucial.

This sculpt tended to confirm the understanding of the family's dynamics already outlined in this chapter. This was quite an emotional, tense part of the session. Jim looked pretty desperate, HM noticed.

What an insecure situation for everyone. Threats of desertion will have considerable power. Are the children testing out the strength of the adults' set-up?

Having a co-worker was helpful here. As planned HM had concentrated on encouraging and observing the sculpt—PO'B had "managed" the sculpt. HM had therefore been in a better position to spot that the time was right to press on to how the family would like things to be.

FIG. 7.2

next to Linda, Linda next to Suzie, Suzie next to himself and Joan on Michael's other side. In fact Linda left the room temporarily and so HM stood in for her and then Mary felt faint and so PO'B stood in for her. (They returned soon afterwards.) Michael at first stood with his hands on his hips but when PO'B referred to this he said "No, I should have them in my pockets". As we "froze" the sculpt for a moment people looked at each other with half grins and warmth. Reviewing this sculpt they all said that this was how it should be. Jim said he would do it with his arms round the group. Joan said Jim expressed feeling more than she did. Suzie was visibly moved by the fact that Michael had put her next to him. She said Michael had feelings and even though he rowed with Jim, he'd miss him if anything happened (e.g. Jim dying). We suggested that it was good to know Michael wanted it like this, as they all did and we commented that it was possible to achieve this. Joan said she thought it would not last—Michael changes his mind too

Comments

We've decided not to worry too much if people disappear briefly. If the session is interesting and relevant enough they'll soon be back out of curiosity alone. It would be so easy to get trapped in "games" playing! Of course one should try to understand non-verbal communication such as leaving the room but we wait until our review of the session to speculate on the meaning (in an interactional sense) of a person's departure. Our systems perspective tends to make us view such departures as expressions of family resistance to change. Usually we do not share this understanding with the family—it may be unhelpful to do so. Perhaps some family members, in the course of a session, need to make space for themselves by taking a short break from the group? (See, for example, Suzie's departure, described on page 108.)

Will the family let Michael be different?

Comments

easily—he was fine for a few days after our last visit and then he relapsed. PO'B said it was far too soon to make anything of any apparent progress.

In this comment PO'B was suggesting that progress would be hard to achieve, that it would take time and effort to overcome the problem—secretly, of course, he hoped they would try and prove him wrong, (à la a paradoxical approach).

We then planned to see Jim and Joan only for the next session (March 14th, at 2 pm.) and then the children after that (March 18th, at 7 pm.—we suggested the parents go out for an hour or so while we met the children!)

We then set up the task for them to work on for the next 8 days (i.e. to cover the period until the meeting with the children). For half the time Michael would be in charge of the TV and would negotiate with the others on who would watch what. For the other 4 days the 3 girls would be in charge. Suzie volunteered to monitor the number of rows produced under the two different arrangements and a "no violence" rule was agreed. We wondered which scheme would be most beneficial as far as the family was concerned. Joan and Jim agreed to go along with this. In addition we said that negotiations had to be carried out in a specific way—only the person holding the cushion we picked from the settee could speak and HM and PO'B demonstrated this. They all happily joined in with this waving for the cushion and speaking only when it was thrown to them. Joan asked why we did this and it was explained that it had many implications—for instance, it helped to reduce aggressive shouting, it encouraged people to listen to each other.

We introduced this in terms of it being further exploratory work but this was not the full story. We were arguing for less of their attempted solution. We were advising that they try the opposite strategy of going with Michael—put him in charge, prescribe the symptom.

We did not anticipate that they would always use the cushion but at least we were getting across the message that they needed to improve their communication channels somewhat. The family found this great fun and it was a pleasant way to wind up the session.

We left shortly afterwards, after a few minutes of social chat.

We both felt that this had been a most useful meeting. Indeed we had to spend some while afterwards overcoming our state of euphoria! The session had largely gone according to plan in spite of Jim having conveniently lost the questionnaires. We were delighted that the family had joined in with the drawings and sculpts so easily (partly the result of us taking the initiative in a confident way). The family had given the impression of enjoying each other, perhaps for the first time in a long while, which we felt was a good indication for progress. We also thought that our original hypotheses had been considerably supported by the material that had emerged.

CHAPTER 8

The Third Session—Working with the Parental Pair

Our next meeting, then, was with Jim and Joan alone. In planning it we had in mind three main thoughts from the previous session:

1. The children seemed unsure of the relationship between Jim and Joan and it could be they were testing it out. (Haley argues that something in the family is making the problem necessary.) If the pair separated the children would not only lose a father but a home also. Could the doubt be eased?

2. Jim seemed rather helpless and not sufficiently involved in family interactions.

3. Jim and Joan were not presenting as a closely-united pair, healthily distanced from the children. The drawings demonstrated this.

In the forthcoming meeting, therefore, our aims were threefold. Firstly we wanted to underline the parental coalition. Secondly we wanted to persuade them that they needed to present a united front to the children in order to achieve peace in the home and thirdly we wanted to make suggestions to them about how to set about this. (In all this we would be going to assume that they *did* wish to remain together, unless they gave us clear indications to the contrary.) Thus we drew up the plan set out overleaf.

Commenting on the plan, we wanted to begin by relating their use of space to their relationship; this is a metaphorical way of discussing problems and even suggesting a need for change. Asking them about the future would help to get away from endlessly going over the past—it implies movement and it gets a discussion going in which blame and criticism have no place. This would also provide a positive atmosphere in which to look at them as a couple (point 3) and it would help us to assess the closeness and strength of their relationship. We would be returning the drawings from the last session and using them to support our thinking that more space was needed between the generations. Under point 4 we would identify with Joan and Jim some possible ways of making changes in Jim's role (from being butler to lover and parent) which would also clarify the parental coalition. We would make a list of whatever tasks they agreed to attempt and leave them a copy of it. Having

Session 3		Responsibility of	
Content		PO'B	HM
1.	Find out where Jim and Joan usually sit; suggest they sit together for the session.		✓
2.	Ask them about how they see the future (given that the children were nearing adulthood).		✓
3.(a)	Offer our impressions of them as a couple in relation to the children— i.e. our view that there was a lack of space between the generations and confusion over parental functions.	✓ Jointly	✓
(b)	Use their own drawings to highlight (a)	✓	
4.	Make suggestions about how they might change things, emphasising the difficulties involved in making any changes (à la Weakland)	✓ Jointly	✓
	e.g. (i) demonstrating unity in various ways,		
	(ii) Jim to "sacrifice" himself by doing less about the house,		make list to leave with the couple.
	(iii) withdrawing to another room to adjudicate on disputes,		
	(iv) banning physical violence and working out sanctions,		
	(v) making Michael responsible for the TV.		
5.	Suggest a few weeks' experimenting and negotiate a whole family session after Easter to review developments.	✓ Jointly	✓
6.	Warn them that after our session with the children (in four days' time) the children may be offering to help about the house more or be referring disputes to them. Obtain the parents' co-operation.	✓ Jointly	✓
7.	(Be attuned to references to ghosts and superstition.)		

fixed the next meeting with them, which would follow our session with the children and would include them all, we would hint that they had nothing to fear from our seeing the children as a separate group and we would enlist their co-operation with anything that might arise out of that session. Finally we would watch for the theme of "ghostly tales". (Actually we did nothing about this subject other than treat it with some indifference. It did not seem to be a problem and we did not wish to elevate it to one.)

On March 14th we arrived at their home on time, to be promptly received by Jim. He and Joan seemed quite relaxed. Joan was in seat 2 and Jim was standing. Before sitting down, HM wondered aloud where they normally sat. Joan said she usually sat in seat 2. Jim didn't give a straight answer but firmly placed himself in seat 5. Both Jim and Joan suggested the family had no set seats, Joan adding that she usually used seat 2. Neither of us felt able to insist that they move to sit together, so PO'B found himself in seat 3(!) and HM in seat 1.

Comments

Insisting, HM felt, might have antagonised them; they would probably see the significance of our remarks later. While keeping the plan in mind, one nevertheless "dances in step with the clients' music", i.e. one remains flexible about the plan, it is more of a map than a rigid track.

PO'B put the family's drawings on the coffee table and vaguely apologised for walking off with them at the end of the previous session. We were now returning them for the family to keep. HM then started the session by saying that we wondered what they intended to do in the future given that, in spite of the troubles now, the children would probably be moving on and away some time soon. Joan grinned "thank goodness" and she and Jim told us of their plan for retiring to be near to the sea. Jim talked of having long connections with the sea ("my heritage"). They confirmed that the children knew about their ideas. HM asked Joan if she minded the prospect of moving to a new area, given that we had understood that Joan had lived most of her life in this area. This did not seem to worry Joan. She said she wasn't very close to her family of origin and anyway she felt so pleased with her relatively short-lived security that moving did not seem a threat.

Signs that theirs' was a stable partnership with a planned future. But somehow this was not coming across to the whole family (or to us) in the whole family meetings; it needed to be communicated and demonstrated to the children.

This led to a discussion about what the couple did together. This was problematic because

Comments

of their shift hours—they could only really spend time together at the weekends. They went to a nearby working mens' club for a drink sometimes and on Thursdays they visited an old couple who were housebound. In relation to going out together, they quickly raised the problem of the children having almighty rows back at home. The neighbours had on occasions reported on the din coming from the house, though not in a complaining way. HM asked if furniture was smashed and people injured. Jim hastened to assure us that this was not the case. Both of us then indicated that perhaps Jim and Joan should let the children get on with it and should refuse to be drawn into the squabbling when they got home. They should try to not get worked up about it themselves if there wasn't actual damage to persons or property. Jim was worried about the children being so verbally vicious to each other—we both agreed that this was quite normal in brothers and sisters. (Later on we came back to this, saying that their difficulties were not unique, that it was a matter of degree really.) Jim and Joan told us about family holidays and day trips to the sea. Joan commented that the girls sometimes weren't interested these days but Michael usually expected to be included.

See Chapter 1 about normal difficulties and problems.

Michael has difficulty in allowing closeness between Jim and Joan?

This gave PO'B the opportunity to refer to the drawings on the table. He talked a bit about the usual coalitions and hierarchies in families and suggested, through reference to their drawings, that their family did not conform to such usual arrangements. We discussed the lack of space there seemed to be between people, which we felt must lead to tension and arguments and, linked to this, the lack of clarity between the parents as a pair and the children as a group. PO'B drew an illustration of a typical family, showing

The aim was not to impart insight as to why they were so, but to look at HOW they were and to redefine the problem as a matter of structure rather than as "badness" in Michael.

Comments

the "executive pair" as a distinct hierarchical rank, thus:

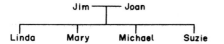

This drawing was not done to impose this model on them but to help them think of themselves as a distinct sub-system.

We wondered aloud whether the children in various ways were getting in between the parents and whether they felt insecure about the future. Perhaps the children were testing things out, including relationships. Joan commented that surely if they liked the present set-up they should behave in order to keep it going. She seemed less happy than Jim about making space between themselves and the children. She talked of how long she had been both mother and father to them and she showed ambivalence about separating a little from them. However, she agreed that *if* she was going to separate she could do so *with* Jim and the children would be able to manage. We advised them to try to avoid threatening to leave (unless they really had decided to go). Concerning the idea that the children's misbehaviour was an aspect of testing out behaviour, HM suggested that if one feels one has a lot to lose this may make one more anxious and hence more likely to test a situation out, if one feels insecure about it in the first place.

Jim felt the main problem was jealousy. We related this to the over-enmeshment of a tangled up family group, where matters of hierarchy and space needed some attention.

At various points in the session Jim and Joan gave us examples of instances where testing out did seem to be occurring and where the family's muddled structure did seem to be creating difficulties and we went over the points made above a few times. This meant we were able to stress the message that Jim and Joan should emphasise their pair alliance and their parental authority. These are some of the instances they reported to us:

The problem is relabelled as a need for a stronger alliance.

1. Michael played games with Jim and Joan over meals. Sometimes he could not decide whether to have lunch or not, which made Joan worried because she felt he should eat regularly. (We assured her that he could do with losing some weight!) Joan's fussing made Jim mad and caused tension between the couple.
2. Joan lent Michael £16 for boots. Jim "played pop" over this. In fact, though, Michael paid her back at £4 per week. Later Jim lent Michael £20 for a bullworker!
3. During a terrible row, involving the whole family, Jim reacted by threatening the whole family with break up. This made Michael even more furious with Mary, whom he blamed for causing this dreadful crisis.

Having obtained agreement from Jim and Joan that their marital and parental relationships needed to be re-affirmed and underlined, we then moved on to suggesting strategies and tasks that might facilitate achievement of these goals. HM noted down a list of suggestions, as they were agreed by everyone, and we left this list with them:

This list amounts to a written contract to perform tasks by which *they* could solve the problem.

"(a) Do things together. Talk about the future together.

This could be much more specific.

(b) Don't get involved in the children's rows.
(c) Don't let the children get you worked up. In difficulties unite, come together.
(d) Don't run round after the children—expect them to do more about the house.

Comments

(e) If pressed to decide the children's arguments, move together to another room to consider the matter.

> Jim was very taken with this idea.

(f) Work out common policies on matters which come up regularly, e.g. should money be lent at all? This makes for problems if Michael, for instance, won't pay up, and anyway it makes for a return to a jumbled family system, e.g. work out a policy on meal times.

> To be policy-makers is to take power.
>
> People sometimes need a face-saving excuse for making a move they've wanted to make for a while. With this list Jim now had an excuse for moving closer to Joan and if Joan felt Suzie was too close to Jim she now had a way of separating them!

(g) Ban violence and work out realistic sanctions. Don't make vague threats about leaving as this raises anxiety rather than calming things. A possible sanction might be to refuse to cook for the offender for a week."

We discussed various examples of how suggestions (a) to (g) might be activated in the home. Jim and Joan indicated that they could see the usefulness of the suggestions and we felt they had a good awareness of the muddle their current practices made for them and the children. Jim was more excited than Joan about these ideas—she had looked almost tearful, earlier in the session, at the prospect of distancing herself from the children. We both recognised her ambivalence about this, saying that she would be bound to feel very close to her children as she'd brought them up single-handed for a time. We also recognised that most mothers regretted their children "leaving the nest" even if they also rejoiced in the prospect of more freedom.

> Mary was about to leave home. While this could well ease sibling tension, it could also be contributing to the problems in so far as a system tends to react to such a change as if it was a major threat.

Jim worried about Michael becoming isolated as he couldn't make friends because he was a bully. PO'B said that it was better to let Michael learn about the realities of life now (by being allowed to experience the consequences of his behaviour) rather than later.

> An encouragement to Jim to be more assertive in his parenting.

Joan commented that she thought that children liked one doing things for them. We explained that, at their ages, they would probably have mixed feelings about this and that anyway they did need to be helped to greater independence. HM suggested that, in adulthood, children worked out new sorts of closeness and warmth with their parents and hinted that this could be just as pleasant. Linked to this was a brief word about Joan's forthcoming grandparenthood. Joan was being teased about her age as a result but Jim said she was really thrilled with the idea of a grandchild. HM emphasised the high status of grandparenthood. (Michael wanted the child to be a boy.)

As planned, we indicated that changes would not be easy to make and we arranged a further meeting with them and the children. Joan wondered if Jim would be available because of his work but he thought he would.

PO'B then in passing asked about how the TV exercises were going. Jim said it was a funny thing but in the first four days there hadn't been any rows. Michael, for instance, had politely asked for certain programmes and had complied with the girls' decisions. (They had been put in charge first.) We said this was very strange/amazing!!

Comments

Joan believed that the more she and Jim did, the more response they should get. They had not appreciated that older children have mixed feelings about dependence.

We wondered if she was more resistant than him and less motivated.
Even though she was suffering a good deal, change might still be resisted (we would say) because of the implications for the system, of which she is a part. (A Freudian might describe her as ambivalent.) Another interpretation might be that such a person sometimes holds on to suffering because it enables them to be weak—a weakness that paradoxically gives them power in that it makes others powerless to help them. Cloe Madanes (1981) develops this notion in her book *Strategic Family Therapy*, Jossey-Bass.

We showed bemused scepticism though we felt like whooping with delight! We took no credit for the change. We didn't, but one could have added that caution was needed about things changing too quickly.

Joan didn't comment on this at first but then she suggested that people had been out a lot anyway.

Joan and Jim asked for our telephone numbers and invited us to write them in their book, under the section marked "Police, Fire and Ambulance"!

As we were leaving, Suzie arrived back from school with her cookery. She said it had turned out badly—Jim teased her about it as he picked up the task list we had made, giving HM a wink as if to indicate that he didn't want the children to see the "battle plans". We also alerted them to the possibility of developments after our session with the children which might pleasantly surprise them.

(Other matters were touched on in the session, but we deliberately gave them little or no attention:

1. Joan mentioned that Jim had two grown-up children. We did not pick up on this.
2. They told us about Michael's offence—it involved him pushing another boy into a river. Michael is a big lad who does not appear to know his own strength when he abuses it.
3. Although Jim claimed he was not superstitious he proceeded to tell us about a ghost horse he'd seen on the road. He said Michael was still afraid of passing the spot.
4. Joan talked a little more about the six months Mary had spent away from home. She'd hit "rock bottom" apparently.)

Comments

Was Joan's comment face–saving? If things were corrected so easily she might feel it implied she had exaggerated the problem, (not that we thought she had.)

This would help to secure their co-operation should the children be offering to do things for them.

This added weight to our argument that violence should be banned.

He seemed to be saying Michael was both a bully and a coward who could be scared (and Jim could handle him?)
All these comments (1–4) could be described as history and by and large we were not interested in it. If aspects of the past do have crucial significance in what's happening *now* then this will become apparent over time and should be picked up and dealt with. Then it isn't "just mere history" but part of the present system.

By the end of this session we had "laid our cards on the table" about our perceptions of the family in a fairly frank way and they had said they could see the logic of our suggestions. Joan and Jim seemed to be going along with what we were recommending, Joan perhaps less so than Jim to whom, it seemed to us, we were giving permission to push for changes.

It may be argued that we did not allow for the possibility of Jim and Joan saying that they really wanted to split up. We felt we had sufficient indications in this session that they wished to remain together (and the content of the previous session had reassured us that the family itself saw a future to its existence). Just because there were problems in the relationship between Joan and Jim didn't "bode ill" for the future—as we've already indicated in Part I of this book, coalition problems and the like are never surprising in families with step-parents.

CHAPTER 9

The Fourth Session—Working with the Children

Our meeting with the children took place four days after the one we had had with the parental pair. We were satisfied that in the session with Joan and Jim we had well underlined their own life as a pair separate from the children and that, to survive, they needed to move closer together. In the coming session with the children, then, we wanted to highlight *their* separateness as a sub-group, which would be partly achieved, of course, by meeting them on their own, and to pursue a number of matters raised and discussed with Joan and Jim.

The plan we drew up for session 4 is set out overleaf.

After enquiring about the TV exercise (which would involve trying to assess the extent of any improvement), we would ask the children how *they* saw the future, both with regard to the management of TV viewing and more generally. We decided that we would raise with them the matters about which Joan and Jim were concerned (point 3) and would try and negotiate ways of overcoming the difficulties that were being reported. As part of this effort to encourage more helpful behaviour we decided that we would actively support the parents' ban on physical violence (PO'B, as the male worker, would lead on this as it might have more impact on Michael) and we would support a ban on the use of the word "bastard" (HM to lead on this as it was the girls who were the offenders). (HM would also try and slot in, for Michael's benefit, a comment on the fact that girls appreciated and were attracted to kindness in boyfriends.) As with the parents, we would draw up a list of agreements and suggestions, a copy of which we would leave with the children. (As we hoped that we would be agreeing with the children that they would do more about the house it had been important to alert Joan and Jim to this possibility at the end of the session with them.) Then we would arrange for the children to be at the whole family session arranged with the parents for a few weeks ahead.

Session 4	Responsibility of	
Content	PO'B	HM
1. Enquire after the TV management exercise. 　—how has it worked out? 　—have they used the cushion? 　—has Suzie monitored the rowing? 　—difference from the base line?		✓
2. What do they intend to do about the TV in future? And the future generally?	✓	
3. What their parents are concerned about. 　—violence 　—squabbling 　—running round after them (Making them unhappy and ill.)		✓
4. What, then, are the children going to do about these matters? (Linked with point 3 and with session with Joan and Jim.)	✓ To support parents' ban on violence	✓ To support ban on use of word "bastard" Jointly to work out list of ways children can help their parents, to render family life more pleasant. HM to prepare written list to leave with the children.
5. Negotiate a whole family session, as with Joan and Jim	✓	

	Comments
We arrived on time to be met by Jim. He said Suzie was on her way and the others were in. With that he and Joan left for . . . , saying they would be back at 8.15 pm. (We'd arrived at 7 pm.) Michael was in seat 2, with his jacket on, collar turned up around his ears. PO'B asked if he'd just come in but he said he'd been in	

for a while. He was watching TV but readily agreed to HM turning it off.

If one has arranged an appointment with people full attention can be expected from them. Taking the initiative, politely, emphasises the "business" nature of the meeting and puts one in charge of things, responsible for the session. (In the next session, we made a tactical error over the TV we think.)

Mary sat in seat 5, her feet curled under her on the settee. Michael shouted at her, "Get your feet down." She refused, snapping back at him. Michael said, "I'm not allowed to do that" to which she retorted that his feet smelt anyway. PO'B asked if slippers were allowed on the furniture but not boots—no clarification was offered.

This sniping seemed to be for our benefit—giving us a hint of what they were capable of?!

Linda joined us, sitting in seat 3. HM took seat 1 and PO'B seat 7. Suzie arrived shortly after we had begun to ask about the TV exercise. She sat in seat 4. When asked about how things had been over the previous eight days as regards the TV viewing, they all agreed that there had been no rows whatsoever and that they had all been able to watch what they had wanted. Suzie in particular tried to minimise this achievement by saying that she had been out most evenings and when it was hinted that the eight day system might continue Linda said it was unfair as Michael had had the weekend part of the week. However, these comments apart, they could not deny the fact that there had not been a single row during the experiment. HM then tried to establish the exact extent of previous rowing. Again the girls, or rather Linda and Suzie, were being a bit difficult by being deliberately vague but Michael said, "every day". PO'B then began to explore for suggestions as to how they could proceed in future so as to be as effective

Like Joan had done in the previous session.

Comments

as they had been in the past week. Suzie was quite grumpy, saying, "we don't have to keep up this carry-on, do we?" Michael, of the four, seemed to be the most willing to seek a line of action—for instance he was willing to go along with the suggestion of alternating weeks, though this was not greeted with enthusiasm by the others. PO'B asked what they thought of giving Michael the responsibility of drawing up a time-table for each week, based on the *Radio Times* and *TV Times*. They did not buy these and we went into a long discussion about how they could not plan on a daily basis and so they needed these planning aids. Mary earned £40 a week, nearly double what Michael and Linda earned, and so she offered to buy them. Michael agreed then to alternate with her. Linda agreed to actually buy the magazines with their money and to provide paper for Michael to draw up a table on which they could all "book" what they wanted to view. Suzie only got £1 a week pocket money and so refused to contribute financially. However, she also got into a heated discussion with Michael about how the whole idea wouldn't work, about the inevitability of conflict if two people wanted different programmes at the same time.

Throughout the session it was Michael who seemed to be happy to compromise, who "stuck his neck out" by offering some contribution in order to get over difficulties. When he did get irritable and unreasonable it was usually as a result of provocation and prevarication on the part of Linda and Suzie especially. It was as if the system, as represented by these two girls, was resisting change. Mary, who was leaving shortly, was more amenable to changes and got very fed up with Suzie at times.

One got the feeling that she would make sure it didn't work! She was really quite aggressive throughout the session, picking fights and interrupting. She said she hated Michael—and didn't respond when reminded of her pleasure when placed next to him in his "ideal family" sculpt. (We had noted that she might have quite an investment in the current "status quo".)

HM terminated the above-mentioned argument by saying that such disputes, if they occurred, should be referred to their parents who would have the final say. This was agreed. (The use of the cushion was briefly mentioned. They had not used it with each other but had tried it on one occasion with Mum. Suzie said Mum had got quite a "shock"—simply because she had not expected the cushion being suddenly thrown at her!)

This linked in with the suggestion made to Joan and Jim that if asked to arbitrate on anything they should retire together to another room to consider the matter. If nothing else this surprises and confuses the people left behind, suspended in the middle of a row!

Comments

HM began a list of the agreements made over the TV (a copy of which we left with the children at the end of the session, once everything was finalised that we had negotiated on.) Below is what was recorded about the management of the TV:

"Michael and Mary on alternate weeks will buy the *Radio Times* and the *TV Times*. (Mary to start.)

Linda will provide Michael with paper so that Michael can plan the week's viewing. People must give Michael their orders and he will work out a plan that's agreeable to everyone. Disagreements that cannot be settled must be referred to your Mum and Jim".

PO'B mentioned that when we had met with their parents we had discussed the future generally, e.g. Mary leaving, and we asked how *they* viewed the longer term. They didn't!! Michael said after a while that he'd never marry. He vigorously "pooh-poohed" the idea of girl friends and marriage but he was grinning as he said this and later on he said that *if* he did ever have children he'd have boys! He said girls were expensive and not worth the trouble. HM worked in the point about girls appreciating gentleness— which developed into a short discussion about what else girls liked in boys. Michael was a bit flippant and shrugged his shoulders but we felt some of the points made got through to him.

> A feature of adolescence or a sign of uncertainty and hence insecurity?

> At one point Michael described his mother and three sisters as "the four girls". More evidence of his inappropriate "parental" position?

Suzie said she would not get married either and Linda stated that if the rows at home continued she would leave home, she wanted to get away as soon as possible. This led on to a good deal of "snarling" at each other with Suzie leading the way! Mary threatened to report Suzie to her mother and tried to bring her into line sharply on more than one occasion.

> Perhaps because of her backwardness, Linda was hard going at times. She got left behind in discussions and "worried" at some matters endlessly. She also seemed to harbour resentments over things in the past, more so than the others (e.g. birthdays that had been forgotten). She kept referring to Michael as the cause of all the troubles—though she did join in on the negotiating.

Comments

As planned, HM shared with the children their parents' concerns—the fact that they were physically violent with each other, that they engaged in endless squabbling and that their parents had to run round after them all in the home. (Linda was a bit "put out" about this last item as she said she helped quite a lot. Joan had, in fact, said she was the most helpful and so we acknowledged this.)

From this point onwards, they tended to argue a lot and to behave just as described—squabbling immaturely! During this period we used one of the advantages of working as a co-therapy pair by talking with each other about their behaviour, saying aloud things like "this is school-kid behaviour isn't it?", "they sound like three-year-olds", "doesn't that sound childish?" etc. This helped to curtail the squabbling, partly because they wanted to hear our discussion with each other! Also, as one of us got caught up in the arguments going on (they often started as reasonable discussions) the other was able to jump in with a comment like "can I draw a line there and move on to . . ." We felt that, without each other, one would have felt hard pressed in this situation and tempted to leave and let them get on with it.

It felt like a performance for our benefit, designed perhaps to test out our ability to bring reasonable control and order to things.

So we avoided getting too caught up in their games-playing, in their typical patterns of interaction. And we did this by doing what we had recommended to the parents—uniting and supporting each other. It also sets a new rule—instead of arguing with them, we talk to them about their game.

Although there was a great deal of unproductive argument, we did also agree on quite a few things. We asked them to consider what changes of behaviour were necessary to achieve the kind of harmony that had been portrayed in the second "ideal" sculpt of our second visit to the whole family. PO'B went round the group, to each one in turn, and as suggestions and agreements were reached HM added them to the list, checking that they were clearly understood.

Thus we tried to present a way of democratically negotiating on matters and communicating clearly with each other.

Michael promised to show no physical violence. (PO'B said we had discussed this with Mum and Jim and that we were supporting them in opposing violence by encouraging them to impose sanctions involving the withdrawal of privileges previously enjoyed in the home. Michael looked startled but took this quietly.) In return for Michael's commitment, the girls agreed not to use the word "bastard". Then they complained of other words that Michael used, e.g. slut, and he promptly promised to cease the practice. (As already mentioned, he was quite co-operative and constructive throughout.) Linda and Mary, in return, were quite amenable to promising not to call him a "puff" in return. (The fact that HM couldn't spell the word they meant produced great amusement.) Suzie, however, would not promise though when we suggested that we were going to record this fact she compromised and said she would not use the word first and would only use it if he insulted her. Linda, when we said we would be asking how they had performed when we next saw them, said she would keep a count of breaches of the agreements.

Even though Suzie was generally sulky and negative she did acknowledge that she was spoilt and "got more". Also, at one point, she commented that she enjoyed "these things", apparently referring to the sessions we were having with them. Even though earlier on she had said to PO'B, when he was confronting her with her awkwardness (she'd said she would get her share of the TV viewing even if she was going to be out!), that he didn't like her. PO'B had replied that he liked them all but didn't think much of their present

Comments

She "wanted it both ways". She was refusing to make changes at first but didn't want this made "public". This would surely have been evidence that the family troubles weren't all Michael's fault? Writing "deals" down clarified things and seemed to contribute to compromise.

Always a useful distinction to make—between a person and their behaviour.

behaviour. (While discussing how immature the "squabbly" behaviour was HM had wondered out loud to PO'B how old Suzie was. We'd decided she was fifteen—PO'B had then said something to the effect of one wouldn't think so, referring to her behaviour. Suzie, who had been listening, had thought he'd meant her appearance and had said, "you should see me all dressed up!")

On several occasions we brought them back to the effect the rows were having on Mum and Jim. Mum had high blood pressure and was seeing a doctor about her heart (Mary thought) and Jim was "proper poorly" with it all. (HM even made a note of this in the list.) We talked about their need to take individual responsibility for their own actions and their consequences. Suzie in particular was bothered about her mother's ill health.

We went on to ask them what activities they could offer to take on or help with in the home. Michael again led off by offering to do the garden and as we went on HM listed the items offered by each person. Below is the rest of the list we drew up with the children:
Michael agrees not to be violent.
Linda agrees not to use the word "b . . ."
Suzie agrees not to use the word "b . . ."
Mary agrees not to use the word "b . . ." while she's at home.
Michael agrees not to use the words "whore", "slut", "slag", "prostitute" etc.
Mary agrees not to call Michael a "puff".
Linda agrees not to call Michael a "puff".
Suzie does *not* agree to not call Michael a "puff" but she won't use the word first.
Linda will keep a check on *if* and how often people do use such words and will report back on our next visit.

Michael will do the garden, on Sundays probably and certainly at the weekend, and will do his own ironing.

Linda will ask her Mum and Jim what jobs need doing regularly. Especially the hoovering.

Suzie will do her own bedroom.

Mary will offer Mum a bit more help in the kitchen and will take a share in cleaning her bedroom. Mary will also offer to cook Sunday breakfast for everyone—so Jim can have a lie in.

A general rule: Take responsibility for your own behaviour and don't try and order other people about.

AND Think of your parents and the effect you're having on them.

With that Joan and Jim returned and our time was up. We fixed up the next meeting as planned and stressed that we would be asking for feedback on today's meeting then. Mary, who hadn't thought that Jim would really want to let her make the breakfast on Sundays, asked him and to her surprise he said "yes, how nice". As we left we commiserated with the parents on their "lot". We indicated that we'd had a hard time keeping the "mob" in order—they seemed amused!

> A fair sharing of family chores helps to untangle roles and to untangle confusion about symmetry and complementarity. This order, concerning domestic tasks, undermines damaging "games", it adjusts the rules. Most dysfunctional families need a session on chores.

> Quite a list!

> And relieved that it wasn't just them?!

The following themes seemed to be in evidence during the session:
(a) These children couldn't resist trying to boss (parent) each other around in a tyrannical way.
(b) Coupled with (a) they seemed reluctant to take responsibility for their own behaviour. There were lots of "blame games".

(c) Coupled with (a) and (b) they were very jealous of what each other was getting. "Everyone should have the same", rather than "to each according to his needs" seemed to be their rather childish approach.

(d) They found it very hard, as one would expect, to stop the endless, circular, unproductive patterns of squabbling resulting from (a), (b) and (c).

(e) However, there was real concern for their mother's health.

(f) They were understandably ambivalent about change. It was convenient in some ways to continue to see Michael as the problem.

Reflecting on the session as we drove away, both of us felt that we had experienced some of the annoyance, frustration and despair that Joan and Jim must feel themselves when interacting with their teenage brood. We had survived because we had stuck to our plan (lights at the end of the tunnel!), had used each other in the ways described on page 96, had remained good-humoured throughout (just!) and had declined to get caught up in their "games". However, we had some doubts as to how effective the session would be in the long run because we had rather "pulled against" the children instead of going with them. Using the children's own momentum would have been more productive but this would have required us to be more devious, subtle and paradoxical. As it was we'd played it "straight" and had been frank and blunt in our comments. Perhaps we'd got it wrong and would need to spend longer on this area? However, on the positive side, the TV task had worked, we'd linked in with the session with Jim and Joan very well and the children had worked quite hard to agree on some matters at least. Moreover, even seeing the children on their own may have helped to re-align the family's structure (especially as Jim and Joan had had to go out on their own in order for the session to take place).

CHAPTER 10

The Fifth Session—Reviewing Developments

So, in the third session we had worked with the parental pair and had agreed with them that they would unite in dealing with the problems. They would try to not get involved in the children's rows, not get worked up by them and they would move to another room to decide on disagreements. They would not run around after the children and would expect more help from them about the house. In the fourth session we had carried on the work with the parents in the work with the children. They had agreed to be more helpful, to undertake a list of chores, to sort out the TV viewing by giving Michael responsibility for planning it and to behave generally in more adult ways.

Our aim for session 5 was to recall with the family that our original contract had been for four sessions, to be followed by a review of progress (if any) to date. Not knowing what to expect, we made a double plan, one to follow if things were much better and another if they were not. (See plan overleaf.)

If the situation proved to be much better, therefore, we would respond along paradoxical lines, showing surprise at *their* success, to provoke them into doing even better. While praising their achievement, we would urge caution about moving too quickly. Our involvement would then be wound down, to a follow-up visit in 6 months' time. On the other hand, it was possible that matters would not be so positive. In that case we would continue with a task-centred approach. We would review their efforts, analysing with them what progress, if any, had resulted from the various tasks, modifying tasks if necessary, continuing with what was helpful and adding a new task to develop family skills in dealing with provocation (by Suzie especially). We would follow this with a session with the parental pair and then a whole family session. But, as with all planning, this was provisional to the extent that we were willing to drop or change points that seemed inappropriate "on the night". In fact on this visit we did not proceed to plan a further full session and we also dropped the mention of a tape-recorder. How do we agree on a change in the middle of a session? We simply stop and address each other directly there and then. If the family asks

Session 5	Responsibility of	
Content	PO'B	HM
1. Remind them of our initial contract and the purpose of this visit—to review things. So, how do they see the problem now?	✓	
2. *EITHER* (a) "Everything's much better"—we express, surprise, caution, scepticism and admiration for their efforts in the face of a difficult situation. (Ask specifically about the TV and household management.)	✓ Jointly	✓
(b) Arrange a follow-up visit in 6 months' time.	✓	
(c) Obtain permission to use material (disguised) for teaching purposes, including publication.		Take a prepared letter. ✓
OR (a) "Some improvement but . . ." or "nothing's changed"—work through the children's task list for more detailed analysis of changes/successes and failures.		✓
(b) Suggest the family keeps working on the tasks agreed with the adults and children for a further three weeks. Add an additional task—to help them practice dealing with provocation —Suzie is to try to provoke family members on their most difficult nights. The family members must deal with this provocation as pleasantly and nicely as possible. We would argue this was a useful skill generally!		✓ Drawing up a further list as appropriate.
(c) Arrange a visit to Jim and Joan (together) as soon as possible and a whole family session for three weeks' time.	✓	
(d) Introduce the use of a tape-recorder, on the grounds that we needed to analyse things in more depth.		✓

what we are discussing, we explain. Usually it is self-evident, e.g. "In view of this, we had better just arrange a visit with Mum and Dad only, and then leave it at that. I think this, what do you think?"

In the event we had considerable difficulty in fixing a time for our fifth visit to the family. On three occasions the session was postponed because Jim had been called out to work late. Originally we had arranged to visit four weeks after the fourth session but a further four weeks passed while we persevered trying to meet up with them. We found this very frustrating and as time went on we began to feel that probably this next visit might well be the last. We thought that if things hadn't improved the family would in all likelihood be "yelling" about it, either to us or Miss Scott. If Michael's behaviour had improved then it was to be expected that our visits would have dropped in the family's list of priorities. And, with all this delay, it would probably be difficult for both the family and ourselves to really "rise to it again", to regain our motivation to get going all over again.

In fact the feedback we were getting from the family when they rang us to postpone the sessions booked was encouraging. On the first occasion Jim had reported that things weren't too bad at home and that, apart from one or two incidents, Michael was much better. He had, apparently, refused to go to Mary's wedding because Jim had criticised what he had been intending to wear to it—he had spent the day in his bedroom sulking. Jim also reported that Michael had refused three choices of meals one day and so he and Joan had not given him anything to eat! When the family rang to postpone the sessions twice more we became anxious even though the family was assuring us that they were finding the sessions helpful and wanted to fix another meeting. So we rang Miss Scott who said she had recently seen Michael on a reporting night. Michael was saying that things were much better at home, that, though he and Suzie were still having words, their words didn't come to anything. Miss Scott herself was very pleasantly surprised with the changes she was seeing in Michael. In early sessions with him she had found him uncommunicative, sulky and apathetic. Now he was initiating topics for discussion with her and was telling her all about his renewed interest in fishing, stamp-collecting and in his job. She had seen Jim a couple of weeks previously, when he had brought Michael down to her office to report, and he was saying that the family were finding the sessions enjoyable and useful. Miss Scott was sure that if there were any troubles at home she would have heard about them. We were reassured!

Eventually it became clear, however, that with Jim's work commitments, we were not going to be able to fix a whole family session for some while. So we decided to cut our losses (perhaps we should have waited?) and visit the family even though Jim would not be available. We also realised that as Mary had married she would probably not be there either. When we rang Joan to confirm this she reported that Michael's behaviour had much improved and that life generally was a lot better, "thank goodness". She was now worried about Mary's continuing bouts of nausea which were affecting her enjoyment of her pregnancy and early married life. So perhaps we were correct— perhaps our visits were no longer so important to the family—after all we could not offer much help with early morning sickness!

Comments

We arrived promptly at 8.15 pm. as arranged and were welcomed very warmly by Joan. On entering the living room we found the furniture had been moved about (we did not comment on this.) The settee was now by the wall and the armchairs were where the settee used to be. In this report we will keep the seat numbers as they were in the room. Therefore, the settee becomes seats 1 to 3 thus:

A change of seating can reflect a change in family relationships, provided one has not prompted it. Here, however, Jim and Linda were out and nothing much could be learned from this change.

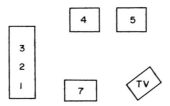

Joan sat in seat 5, Suzie was in 4 and Michael in 2/3. HM sat in seat 1 and PO'B in seat 7. Jim was at work and Linda was out. Joan said she was not sure where Linda was, Michael said she had been in and out.

The TV was on and Suzie and Michael seemed engrossed in it. They assured us it would finish shortly and so we agreed to leave it on until the end of the programme.

We were giving in to them, condoning a breach of our contract to make a working visit. We were making an error, giving Suzie and Michael power they should not have.

Meanwhile Joan was knitting. She reported that Jim was at work. Suzie was eating and, after working her way through a bowl of cereal, decided to make herself a sandwich. Then Joan made us a cup of coffee, which we accepted. Michael, who was naked from the waist up and sat hugging a cushion, asked for tea.

Had the cushion any meaning? We had used it to signify who was empowered to speak. But he seemed to be hugging it as a child hugs a teddy. He also used it to conceal smirks of enjoyment in the session and by lowering it he could display his manly chest, the result of his body building.

Suzie, whom Joan had asked to put the kettle on, said she wouldn't make tea for Michael and Joan immediately said she would make his!

Although the TV programme was still on, things had been disturbed by our arrival and, in fact Michael, rather than watching the show, chatted with HM about his taking up of stamp collecting and fishing. He discussed particular stamps etc. and was very forthcoming and relaxed during this period—a more confident, mature person. Suzie had one or two digs at him, to which, to his credit, he did not rise.

Once the programme had finished the TV was switched off and PO'B, as planned, set the scene for the session by reminding them of our original contract and suggesting that we review things now. When he asked how the problem was now he looked at Joan. She was about to answer when Suzie, who looked fairly defiant and sullen throughout, made sure to get a quick "much worse" in. Joan, however, was encouraged to continue and she reported that things had greatly improved. Michael had behaved in more reasonable ways and there had not been the old rows over the TV programmes. There had been one or two incidents related to his refusal to go to Mary's wedding but overall she seemed to be feeling that life was more pleasant in the home—until today, that is, when Michael and Suzie had been niggling at each other all day.

Michael and Suzie then proceeded to give us a demonstration of this—calling each other names, making sure they always had the last

Comments

Suzie getting the game going or perhaps Michael had made the first move (asking for tea). Joan takes the easy way out—if she was tired she was being a willing martyr. However, both Suzie and Joan would blame Michael for any upset caused.

Showing no interest in the TV and indicating thereby that the request to watch it was a matter of getting his own way. Suzie too was more interested in sniping at Michael than watching TV.

Suzie attempting to disqualify us? She has an investment in things not changing—she benefits by Michael being the "baddy".

This had been mentioned earlier; the refusal could have been provoked by Jim. Interesting how many problems surround changes in the family life cycle!

Was this because we were coming and a show of conflict was worked up for our benefit? On the other hand it was an oppressive, thundery day and we wondered if that had affected their mood.

Comments

word, blaming each other for the problems. Michael was not blameless but Suzie provoked as much as she was provoked, probably more. One certainly had the impression that she instigated the whole "to do" this particular evening. Joan seemed aware of this and, rather unsuccessfully, used pleading, threats and anger to control them both.

Showing that what was probably her usual "attempted solution" was ineffective.

We wondered aloud with each other why Michael and Suzie were putting on such a show for us and in the course of the one and a half hours' session a number of reasons were suggested:
(a) they were doing it for our benefit, for some reason,
(b) Michael was "winding up" because, apart from him and Linda, the family were going away on Saturday for a week to Cornwall. (Michael and Linda were at work.)
(c) The weather was stifling and humid, putting people on edge.

This distances the workers from the squabbles and it breaks a common dysfunctional rule that "the rules (of an interactional sequence) are not discussed". Breaking such a rule helps to produce a better one.

Joan commented that Jim hated it when Michael and Suzie rowed like this—he thought it was dreadful that a brother and sister should carry on like this. Joan too thought it odd that they should be so hateful as they were full brother and sister. HM remarked that rowing between children in a family is quite normal, though these two seemed to be carrying on a child-like habit into adulthood inappropriately.

Relabelling the behaviour as childish.

When we did interrupt Michael and Suzie in their games-playing they seemed unworried by the unpleasant things they were saying to each other and they grinned quite cheerfully when we commented on this.

They were enjoying the effect the rows were having.

It became clear that it was Joan (and presumably Jim) who suffered from the upset, noise and sheer wearing effect of it all. It *was* wearing and we sympathised with Joan and pointed out the effect of their behaviour to Michael and Suzie.

So what to suggest? As a beginning, PO'B asked Suzie to move to sit next to Michael. She refused. HM got up quickly, saying she would swap seats with her and Suzie too, almost involuntarily, got up and swapped with HM. Suzie sat as far away as possible from Michael, in seat 1. PO'B asked her to move up to seat 2, saying he wished to join them on the settee (in seat 1.) Suzie and Michael commented on each other's smell (negatively!) but otherwise sat giggling. We then tried to get them to row with each other again. They were incapable of doing so. They said they could not row to order and that it was harder when you were sitting next to someone. Everyone was laughing quite good-humouredly at this point—including Joan. We wondered with Joan whether this was one way to deal with their quarrelling but she was sceptical about them moving together for her. She then moved to seat 7!

Then, as we were addressing ourselves to Joan, aggressive behaviour developed between Suzie and Michael who ended up "scrapping" with each other on the settee. PO'B and Joan had to intervene quite forcefully to physically separate them.

Comments

It was the rule—"Rows upset Mum and Jim"—that gave the rows meaning and drew Joan and Jim into them, thus creating a vicious circle because the more they tried to solve the rows the more they were encouraged. Our suggestion, in the visit to Joan and Jim, that they separate from the rows and physically move to another room, was correct.

To make it harder for them to row. This confident initiating of action is powerful. It is also a model for parents, counterpointing as a united pair.

Prescribing the problem behaviour is (paradoxically) a way of controlling it. It institutes a second order change and starts a new game.

We are not sure how the fight started but Joan's move to seat 7 meant we were not watching the children as we spoke with her. Nevertheless, it was an error on our part to leave them for those few moments. But Palazzoli would say errors are more instructive than success (if recognised). If we

Comments

were to do it again we would ask them to return to their seats before discussing their failure to row! By turning away from them we lost some of our control. Perhaps if we had not given in over the TV viewing they may not have made this latest bid for power?

Suzie then disappeared to the toilet, returning shortly afterwards to the lounge in her nightwear. Michael, who was quite worked up by now, started making very rude comments about Jim, calling him the "fancy-man" and hinting about damaging information he had about Jim that was contributing to the problems. PO'B said firmly that we were not interested in that sort of old history but what people were doing to each other now.

See page 78 for a few comments on the significance of such disappearances.

To allow him to continue using this threat would be giving him inappropriate power.

Michael repeated things he had said before about his mother. He said her first loyalty should be to him, not Jim. We pointed out that Joan would be silly to choose Michael while his behaviour was such, in contrast to Jim who provided her with a comfortable life for the first time in her life. Michael repeated threats to use violence to get his own way and for a while reverted to his most difficult, unreasonable behaviour. Suzie too, when she returned, talked of fighting her way through difficulties, e.g. at school, and she argued that her mother had told her to stick up for herself when she was little. Joan replied that such behaviour was now inappropriate at her age.

This was all rather tiresome but, on reflection, it is important not to over-react to it—it *does not* mean that there is no progress, as we learned in the next session.

Joan was feeling exasperated and pretty hopeless by this stage in the interview (so were we!) She commented that we must think she was a liar when she was reporting that things were much better. She said that when things have got as bad as this in the past she

Comments

and Jim have threatened to get Michael out, e.g. by calling the police. She said in a surprised tone that she sometimes thought that Michael wanted her to carry out her threat.

Indicating that our concern was to help Joan, we went on to try and identify strategies that she and Jim might use to control things, for their own sakes. We made it clear that we were not bothered about Michael and Suzie rowing as such—we were very concerned, however, about the effect it had on the adults.

It would have been very easy to get bogged down here but we managed to make Mum the focus of the intervention, i.e. the client. It was she who had the problem and who needed to be helped to not get upset.

Privately, of course, we did bother about the strength of the negative feelings and violence between Suzie and Michael but we felt that trying to stop them rowing only served to increase it.

We suggested Joan watch the TV upstairs, swapping the colour and the black and white models. The children hated this idea and anyway Joan said she could still hear them arguing downstairs. We suggested she and Jim insist they go outside to row but various obstacles were put up against this idea—the neighbours, the children refusing to go. We noticed that Joan seemed to be feeling that putting them out was a very final thing. She could not see the possibility for variations on the "time out" periods. She said Michael may have to leave when he was eighteen. We suggested that he need not leave finally, but only until he was willing to behave. She wanted him to behave like an adult—yes, we thought to ourselves, but she still babies him or acts as his slave?

Actually this was not a good sanction. Rather than requiring a member to do something, it is much easier to withdraw a service from them, e.g. cooking for a grown-up child.

Perhaps she could only see the difference between total rejection and total permissiveness, not the blends of control and freedom in between—a problem for many parents.

While we discussed these matters with Joan, the children looked on interestedly, making protests at various points, but not getting back to their "games". Michael took seriously the fact that we were supporting Mum and Jim and would be discussing sanctions with them when we next met them. He said

Comments

he would be present when we did this but we made it plain that he would be asked to leave.

At this point we had hinted that our next visit would be to Joan and Jim alone, to back them up as a parental pair. (Seeing them alone does that in itself, symbolically.)

We then began to wind up the visit by arranging a time for the next visit/session with Joan and Jim only, to discuss strategies and sanctions. We agreed to make it June 24th (in 19 days' time.) At this point Suzie twice commented that she wished *we* were her parents, for a week at least, so we could sort them out! We did not argue that this was silly, but let it go with a smile. (We wondered whether she was asking for limits. Having too much power can be uncomfortable for a child.)

Palazzoli discusses this odd move, i.e. the client suggesting the worker can only help by being someone else. She suggests that two counterparadoxes are needed:
(a) connote the message as right,
(b) tell ourselves to comply, as it is necessary to the therapy!

Such people want to change reality. They are dealt with by saying "we have to change the past for you—to make ourselves what your parents are not. We don't know how we will do it but we will try". It is hoped that this will cause them to think, "we mislead you—how could you be our parents—but we appreciate the offer."

By the time we left calm had returned.

There were other points mentioned in the session:
1. Mary was all right. Marriage was suiting her. She was settled and had lost her aggressiveness. She and her husband visited occasionally. Michael now related well to the latter who was a karate expert!
2. In discussing Michael, Joan pointed out that he was great with a little boy who called round. Michael was hoping Mary's baby would be a boy. He was probably feeling outnumbered by the women.
3. Joan said Jim now took Michael to report to his probation officer—she thought that the lifts in the car helped the regularity of his reporting. We would see the offering of lifts by Jim, and their acceptance by Michael, as a sign of progress towards a more functional family—towards more positive parenting. Michael had been seen as a "parental child" (seeking symmetry with the adults)—accepting a lift from Jim showed a return to complementarity.
4. From her comments, we suspected that Suzie was a handful at school.
5. Despite the upsets during this visit, we noticed that Joan was looking very fit and well. She was far more relaxed, alert and smiling than when we first met her.

As we came away from the house we commented on Michael's show of maturity at the beginning of the session, although his later lapse was depressing for a time. Suzie had been at her most difficult. Still, Joan had reported big improvements, except for that night. She still found it difficult to be tough to control them—perhaps she feels guilty about the early, unsettled life she gave them? Because of the errors we had made we had struggled sometimes but we have come to believe that not only do we learn skills through our errors but also we can learn much about a family by getting it wrong with them at times. We can often turn the error to advantage, saying to the parents, for instance, "see what happened when we . . ." or "like all parents, we make mistakes, but these show up what changes might be considered".

In the event, we had done what we thought we would do if things were not sufficiently satisfactory, i.e. arrange a further visit with Joan and Jim. In this difficult session, the support of a co-therapist was a real life-line. As regards following the plan, the main diversion occurred when we held back from recommending tasks and especially the additional task of getting Suzie to be provocative so that the others could learn how to respond. This was partly because we had now realised even more clearly how the problem and solution lay with the parents. In task-centred work the task is assigned to those who have an acknowledged problem and in this family this hardly included the children. So our main work would be with the adult pair. Also, we felt it might have been better to ask them to try such an exercise while we were with them, i.e. in the session, in place of asking them to row. But, one has to do some quick thinking on one's feet, even within a closely-thought-out plan, and no one does the best thing every time!

CHAPTER 11

The Sixth Session—A Final Meeting with the Parental Pair

Since the previous session PO'B had been in telephone contact with Miss Scott. It concerned an interesting telephone conversation she had had with Jim just prior to the family's departure to Cornwall for their holiday. Jim had asked Miss Scott to keep an eye on Michael and Linda. He and Joan did not want any trouble and they were worried that their holiday could be "messed up" (their last one was because their car had broken down). Jim was indicating that if Michael caused trouble, like hitting Linda, they would hear about it and come racing back. We felt this was a classic example of Jim and Joan (a) getting too involved and (b) more importantly, giving Michael the power to wreck things and perhaps not giving him an opportunity to behave differently. We realised that Jim must have intended to ring home to check up on things because as they were moving about from place to place (using bed and breakfast vacancies) Linda and Michael could not have rung them. No wonder, we thought, trouble starts, given this sort of invitation!

We thought Jim and Joan were still doing the sorts of things we had counselled them against and that they were not keeping too well to some of the tasks we had suggested. Therefore we saw it as our aim, in the next meeting, to reinforce what we were saying when we last met them alone, without making them feel criticised and failures as parents and without trying to impose our understanding and solutions on them, which, of course, would have little effect unless they agreed with our perceptions.

The plan we drew up for the visit is set out on the next page.

In points 1 and 2 we hoped to turn our own error to advantage by using it to show them how we can all get it wrong and how we can learn from mistakes. We would emphasise that "it is not easy", in order to show them that we were not criticising them but that we were all working it out together. Point 3 would lead to more of these ideas. Point 4 would ease us into reviewing tasks and encourage them to keep up with the plan. As regards point 5 we thought that withholding the cooking of meals would be easy to carry out and would be a move towards increasing the children's responsibility. On point 6, we were not sure about future contact—it would depend on

112

Session 6	Responsibility of	
Content	PO'B	HM
1. Discuss the last (fifth) session where we felt we went wrong—how we let Michael and Suzie take control and thus how we had a hard time. The children were not upset, the adults were!		✓
2. We would then say we were reminded of our earlier meeting with Jim and Joan alone, where we had decided that the children acted up *for the adults' benefit*. So all 4 of us had fallen into the trap of giving the children the chance to misbehave. PO'B would mention his telephone call with Miss Scott—another example of giving children control—and would ask, "what if it had been handled differently?"	✓	
3. So, we would ask, how did the holiday go?		✓
4. We would comment that the children themselves seemed to want firm limits set—we would mention Suzie's remarks and Michael's amenableness to firm action? Now the children were nearing adulthood, the parents needed to be more devious in their handling and, of course, it would not be easy. We would ask Joan and Jim how far they had followed the list of suggestions we drew up together at our last visit?	✓ Jointly	✓ done
5. Go through the list. What about the "row outside" rule? We would say we suspected that if the parents refused to get involved in the rows, the chance of anything serious happening would be greatly reduced (though there was no real damage to people or property as yet, anyway). We would say, "don't try and make them be nice to each other, just refuse to let them get you upset and apply firm sanctions, (e.g. no meals), to stop them from bothering you".	✓ Jointly	done ✓
6. Plan any future contact.	✓	
7. Obtain agreement to use the case for teaching purposes etc.		✓

how they felt and what gains we would all settle for. We thought we were nearing the close, however, and therefore point 7 would involve us asking their permission to use their case for teaching and publication purposes—to this end we would take a prepared letter for them to sign.

Our aims could be summed up thus:

(1) Using the dynamics of the previous session and their handling of Michael during their holiday, we would encourage them to keep to the tasks and to be subtle in avoiding becoming upset.

(2) We aimed to wind up our involvement if things were reasonably well under control and relationships progressing.

(3) We aimed to get approval for the use of their experiences in our other work and to negotiate a follow up contact if we wished to check how they were.

Comments

We arrived a few minutes late. They were finishing lunch and we waited while Joan made tea (the kettle seemed to take ages to boil). While we were waiting we got chatting to Jim about the holiday and he said he had enjoyed it and the car had given no trouble. Joan was pleased that Michael and Linda had missed her. They told us Joan had been to the hospital today for one of her regular check-ups. We did not ask for details but they gave us the impression that nothing was bothering them as a result of her tests. Wimbledon was on TV and when Joan joined us with her tea she sat next to HM who suggested that we switched off the TV to which they replied "Yes, please do". HM, who was nearest to the set, switched it off. PO'B was in seat 5 and expected Jim to take seat 4 but he sat on a dining chair behind 4. HM was in seat 1 and Joan in seat 3/4. PO'B had to sit sideways to see Jim.

We made no comment on this—Jim still keeping himself on the periphery, a bit?

HM began by recalling the last visit, how we had been analysing it and had decided that we had made a mistake by allowing Michael and Suzie to watch the end of the TV show.

This had given them power, inappropriate to their place in the hierarchy, which had invited trouble. We reflected on this for a time with Jim and Joan, on how Michael and Suzie "play up" for the adults' benefit and how we had fallen into the trap of giving them a chance to be difficult. We discussed how they (the children) seemed to be doing two apparently contradictory things, (i) behaving childishly by demanding mothering, e.g. extra cups of tea and (ii) taking over as "boss" of the house. We encouraged them to respond to reasonable requests while not giving the children the power to rule—to try to steer Michael on the middle course towards becoming a responsible grown up son.

PO'B then introduced his conversation with Miss Scott and how, in discussing it, we felt like contacting Jim to suggest he avoid ringing home as this gave Michael the power to wreck the holiday by simply upsetting Linda. As it happened Michael had behaved himself while they were away even though they had rung home two or three times a week. Jim explained that he had had to ring in case there were urgent messages for him from work or in case the police were harassing Michael. Jim then told us that he had a very serious talk with Michael before the family had set off and he had told Michael, in the strongest terms, that if they had to come home because he had started something, he (Michael) would be put out and would have to stay out—"the permanent boot", Jim called it.

Jim gave us the impression that he had really convinced Michael that he had meant it. Jim told us he had meant it, so we commented that it looked as if he had pitched it right and

Comments

Both possibilities were unlikely.

We wondered if this was too severe—an all or nothing situation. Would Jim enforce this threat? We would come later to more realistic sanctions, like doing less for Michael.

Teenage children respond well to reasonable firmness. Perhaps the earlier progress towards complementarity, aided by making space between the hierarchical that Michael had responded because he had known where he stood.

Joan was really pleased that Michael and Linda had missed her and she was relieved that they had managed together. They had continued to baby-sit for a single neighbour who worked beyond her child's school hours. Michael had made coffee for this neighbour each evening.

Then, after going off for a while at various tangents with Jim repeating a great deal of what he had told us previously, we moved on to asking about their general strategy for dealing with trouble in the home. They still had the list we had left them when we saw them earlier on as a pair but they admitted that they had not always followed it. Even so, life was very much better and there had been no problems since our last visit. While Joan said Michael and Suzie were "fifty-fifty at fault", Jim said Michael started any trouble eight to nine times out of ten. He had seen him walk past Suzie and deliberately kick her foot, saying "mind your bloody foot". When this happens Jim says to Michael "I saw that—cut it out" and he seems to respond. Jim chatted about how he drives Michael to his fishing and how he helps him with his pools. He also reported that he had received £1 each from Suzie, Michael and Linda for Father's Day. Michael and Linda had bought identical cards for Jim but Michael had maintained that his was better as he had bought it first!

Comments

ranks, had enabled Michael to accept his place. At this point we felt it was important to accept and support Jim's intention to get more involved and hence what he did, even though we had some reservations about the actual strategy he used. An example of Minuchin's "tracking".

A considerable shift in her view of Michael.

A nice sign of movement away from being a parental child?

Comments

We gained the impression that Jim had greatly increased in confidence as a parent. He seemed to be intervening appropriately and positively and he was coupling being assertive in discipline with being fatherly in offering lifts, sharing Michael's interests etc.

Both Jim' and Michael's actions showing complementarity.

We underlined again for them that we felt they had got the knack and that it may help to recall the main points on the list we had drawn up with them from time to time, i.e. not to let themselves get worked up by the children's rows, not to tolerate trouble, to tell Michael and Suzie to go outside if they had to fight, to leave the room if they stayed and still rowed but to say that it was very inconvenient and that (as a sanction) no meals would be cooked for either of them for a week. Since the children fought for the impact it had on the adults, Jim and Joan had to be sure to separate from it rather than get drawn in trying to stop it.

The opposite to the "more of the same" method used in the past—and a change in the nature of the game—fighting now sends the parents away to unite.

HM commented that since Michael and Suzie were no longer little ones, Joan and Jim might have to be more devious (illogical—doing the opposite to the expected) in managing them. This is what we had done in asking Michael to be in charge of the TV viewing timetable. Jim confirmed that that move had been very successful and that there were no more rows over television. Jim thought that some of the success over the TV was due to people's working hours resulting in few occasions when two people wanted different programmes.

The power is with who decides who is in charge!

Success in this area had been self-rewarding and had shown that they could function in more satisfactory ways if they thought about it. He is throwing a little disqualification our way! We will counter this by saying that it is them (not us) who have solved the problem.

Discussion then rambled off again down familiar lanes that we had travelled along earlier and PO'B said he was wondering about how to round off the session. Overall, he said, there was a great improvement, with the exception of Michael not attending the wedding and the scene on our last visit, Joan and Jim seemed to have made considerable progress in handling the situation, while Michael was nowhere near as much a problem for them as when we started. "Would that describe it?" PO'B asked. Jim said he had grave doubts, when we started, about whether talking could change things, but he had to admit, he said, "and I'm not saying it just because you're here", that our visits had made a great improvement. They were definitely over the worst. We said we were pleased to hear that but we felt change was due to family members being willing to make small changes in behaviour, rather than due to any magic on our part or in our words.

PO'B said it looked, in view of the favourable state of things, as if this could be our final visit. We asked how they felt about ending our involvement at this stage. Both again expressed satisfaction with the present and confidence about the future. Joan commented that no doubt the family would have its ups and downs in the future—"What family doesn't?", she said. However, the overall impression was that things were a bit more manageable/copable with, as it were. We again reminded them to focus on some apparently minor things as a way to future success, e.g, not doing too much for grown-up children, like running round after them making them cups of tea.

Joan and Jim knew Miss Scott was leaving the probation service and they expressed a wish that Michael should remain under supervision, especially as he might need some support when his youth opportunities job ended shortly, to make sure his job satisfaction needs were not neglected. We suggested they link up with Miss Scott about this.

Further informal chat followed and Jim asked us again about where exactly we were based and did we train people like Miss Scott. We explained our work and this gave us an opening to ask their permission to use their case for teaching purposes etc., provided it was thoroughly disguised. They gladly agreed and signed a prepared letter, Joan saying, "I'll be your first witness". Jim offered us paper from his work when he learnt about the economic cuts at our workplace, but we did not encourage this!

We then made an agreement with them that, by way of follow up, we could ring them any time.

In another, more recent case, we've "banked" a session with the family in case it's needed. Weakland *et al.* suggest this is a way of extending one's therapeutic influence.

We expressed mutual pleasure at working together. Mary's name came up and they told us how, since being married, she had lost her bad temper and was much more pleasant. Jim wondered if the rapid progress in the family would have occurred if she had not left home. We said we felt her going probably would have helped the changes. It was healthy for the young ones to leave the old nest! Joan and Jim said Michael and Mary now got on much better.

One could speculate that it was her pending departure, hastened by her pregnancy, that was really disturbing the system, leading to Michael being scapegoated, and that things would have settled down without therapy. It is interesting how often such explanations come up afterwards. We think they would have needed help—the family needed help to untangle itself and correct the "parental child" role of Michael.

As we left HM commented on the change of seating and they said Linda had done that.

We have noticed before that sometimes it is a backward sibling who is the most sensitive to the dynamics of a family—even though not participating much verbally, she had made a significant contribution to change or, to put it at its least, had expressed that change and her acceptance of it.

We exchanged warm good-byes and left.

We believed we achieved significant change. Here are the gains made:

1. Michael's behaviour was no longer a serious problem to them.
2. Michael's behaviour *had* matured/improved in various ways. He was less of a parental child.
3. Joan and Jim had learned better ways of coping with him and the other children and were more confident about handling things in the future.
4. Jim and Joan had clarified and strengthened their parental functioning and Jim had got more involved, both in matters of discipline and in more positive fatherly activities.
5. The risk of family break up was reduced. Life was tolerable and, to some extent, pleasurable for them all. Joan was looking much better—younger even.

These gains exceeded our expectations at the referral stage. To press on would have met our needs more than the family's. It is important not to do even a little too much but it is very tempting not to leave people one has grown to like!

CHAPTER 12

Conclusion

Palazzoli and her colleagues (1978)[1] comment that therapists must study the "moves" of the family, as one studies a chess opponent. They must respect the skill of the family, learn to laugh at defeat and admit "They're fantastic players"! In other words, plan well for every encounter and scale down your pride. Practise hard, as a David taking on a Goliath; be ready to lose but meanwhile enjoy the stimulation of the challenge.

But families greatly differ from chess players in that they have painful disorder in their lives. Having a clear method for setting aims and devising plans for each intervention help to bring order to the therapists' minds. This order seems to get picked up by the family members who are thereby helped to establish some order in their complex interactions.

In Part I of this book we presented our selection of those theories that *work* for us in our own practice, with families referred to us by probation officers. We have attempted to sum up those parts of the literature that help us to explain the family problems we encounter and that offer a method for dealing with them. We have illustrated our outline with as many practical examples as possible, including our presentation of our work with the Green family in Part II of the book. Our work with the Greens also demonstrates our method of planning each session. We hope this will be seen as an almost routine method which, if employed by any worker, will lead to productive therapy, without the need for any "special charisma" (though, no doubt, this helps too!). It is our conviction, however, that having a partner greatly enhances the planning and implementation of work, especially for beginners, a point we will return to later in this chapter.

Reflecting on a few of the mainstays of our approach, we would like to make the following comments on the key elements in our approach:

A. *Systems orientation* Systems thinking, ideas of interactional sequences and the notions of sub-systems and structures help to give us dimensions for understanding families and their problems. These ideas assist us to develop hypotheses and hence form the basis on which strategies for interventions are developed, e.g. task designing which will serve to underline the parental coalition, make space between hierarchical ranks, restore a parental child to complementarity with parents (and symmetry with siblings).

At a conference one of us attended recently (1981)[2] Peggy Papp suggested that the therapist needs to ask him/herself the following four questions:

(a) What function does the symptom (presenting problem) serve in the system?

(b) What is the cycle of interaction in the family maintaining the symptom? (Looking at the family's attempted solutions will tell one a good deal.)

(c) What would be the consequences of change?

(d) Where will the greatest resistance come from?

We think these are useful, orientating questions to ask oneself.

B. *Changing beliefs* This is also referred to as reframing, relabelling. These are common ways by which a family's belief system can be altered. "Positive connotating" is a more paradoxical strategy for relabelling symptomatic behaviour. In our work with the Green family we did not use what could be called a "major reframe", although some relabelling of people's conduct took place. We would like here to mention again the family we referred to in relation to scapegoating in Chapter 1. In this case a major reframe was the centre of our earliest intervention with the family. Repeating the family details given earlier, the Brown family had a fifteen-year-old daughter who was disruptive at home and at school. The school was on the point of excluding her. Her parents were very distressed (both were on "nerve" tablets) and were barely coping with her. She was staying out late, sometimes all night, she was defiant to the extent that they were suggesting she would have to go into "care" and the probation officer was concerned that this might be the outcome. She felt she was having no impact and that the real problems lay in the family. She had no doubts about the girl's mental state though the school was suggesting she was "psychiatric". On our first visit, having satisfied ourselves that there was a circular "cause" to the difficulties, a spiral of inappropriate reactions (with the parents applying more and more of a "solution" that was "causing" the girl's problems to grow), we offered them this reframe (drawing on Cade's example (1980),[3] already referred to in Chapter 4):

Towards the end of a long session exploring family problems one of us said in the hearing of the whole family, "Finally, I want to say that this kind of problem with teenagers is very common—we see a lot of it nowadays. It *is* hard on parents—we really do sympathise with you and we know it is hard to bear. Some children are worse than others and can be *so* difficult to tolerate, *so* argumentative and problematic. It takes some coping with. But there is a reason for it though you may find this hard to accept. At about this age, when children are near to taking that big step from childhood into adulthood, of moving from being childish to becoming responsible and caring (for themselves included), they may become very fearful of taking this step. They are scared to take on responsibility for themselves and so they continue to act childishly. What parents naturally tend to do is to demand more mature behaviour, but this is an error. It makes the child feel he or she is being rushed into taking this fearful step and so he or she panics and becomes even more childish. Therefore our advice is (A.) try not to rush her from childishness into more adult behaviour, instead (B.) help each other to put up with her and understand her. She will take the big step from childishness to responsibility when she is ready, i.e. when she is no longer scared, but not before that. The change can be sudden, so watch her carefully, without interfering and support each other through it". In this reframe we seemed to be going with the symptomatic behaviour and implied that we were encouraging it. We were saying the girl's behaviour was normal (at least for some children who were scared of growing up!) and we were seeking to show the parents that to try and change it would make it worse, through increasing the fear. We implied that a change would soon happen and that they needed to watch for it. (We hoped that they would begin to notice some of the positives in her behaviour which were already there, thereby interrupting the vicious circles of interaction that had been set up.) Meanwhile no teenager wants to be described as "childish". But because we did not attack her or accuse her of being childish (we addressed ourselves to the parents) she was challenged to behave differently, rather than encouraged to argue against us. (We noticed in fact that as we "played" this reframe the girl sat speechless in her chair, with her mouth dropping open!) The parents were most impressed by our analysis of the problem and the intervention really took the "heat" out of the situation. The girl's behaviour improved and anyway the family did not see her as such a problem as before. (The success of the reframe moved us quickly to a major area of dysfunction in the family, the functioning of the parental and marital pair—indeed we moved so quickly that the family system resisted the rapidity of change and we had to work hard to stay engaged with the family. We'll return to this shortly.)

Sometimes, of course, therapists need to reframe their own beliefs about what is normal in families, in order to allow for the wide variations in family life patterns. We are reminded of Marianne Walters' comments[4] at a recent conference about single parent families. She made the point that, in spite of the rapid increase in the proportion of one parent families in the U.S.A. (and over here), people still view such families as weakened, broken, lacking, likely to fail. Certainly economic and social circumstances are stacked against such families but she was concerned that such families begin to view themselves as doomed to failure, because they are not whole. Such negative self-images will only serve to reduce the likelihood of them coping with everyday life problems. Marianne Walters suggested that therapists should counter such families' pessimistic views of themselves by pointing out and building on their internal and external strengths and resources. But, of course, this means that the therapists must approach such families with optimism and a commitment to building the future with the family, rather than with a feeling that whatever might be achieved can only be "second best" to a two-parent family.

C. *Task setting* For every problem that presents itself, we try to work out a problem-solving task which aims to deal with the problem and the sequence of interaction maintaining it. This is an activity in which the family, or a sub-system of it, has to engage. Then it is quite natural that we should say "it is *you* who have solved the difficulty". This reduces the risk of their disqualifying us by relapsing. Strange as the theory may seem, families do appear, in our experience, to have an extraordinarily "perverse" tendency to disqualify one's best efforts. Perhaps this is partly the reason why some workers lose heart in this work. We hope we have encouraged the reader not to be put off! Tasks seem to pay off even if they are often not all that well-implemented. They seem to have the effect of reducing problems to the manageable and a manageable problem almost ceases to be a problem. Don't forget too that small gains, which make people feel even a little more competent, are likely to have spiralling, positive reverberations.

D. *Resistance to change* Do remember that families as systems have inbuilt homeostatic controls. Families will devise ways of throwing off a therapist, e.g. by a flight into health, by disqualifying the therapist, or, as in the Brown family situation mentioned earlier, by developing a reason for asking one to stop visiting. (Mrs. Brown suddenly became so upset/depressed that she had to get medication for a near "nervous breakdown". She tried to stop us visiting them a second time through various roundabout means. We responded by accepting what she was saying but we visited as planned, saying "we thought we would call to see how you were". Using "kid gloves" we eased ourselves into the session, expressing so much concern [which was genuine] that we were not asked to leave. Indeed we were readily asked back.) Holding on to a family takes a certain persistence. This is done in the knowledge that the family will benefit, in the same way that a child will benefit from going to the dentist! BUT, of course, peoples' rights must be respected and only polite persuasion and concerned persistence are acceptable. The understanding that it is normal for a system to resist change helps one to be patient and tenacious in holding a family engaged in therapy. Resistance has to be faced with Mueller's[5] "powerful, committed and optimistic orientation" but also, we would suggest, with a lightness of touch that goes along with the momentum of the family. In effect one is getting the message across that "Yes, we accept all that you are saying, but we will stay with you out of concern and both you and we will survive the contact". Our moral justification for this persistence is based on the facts that a contract has been made with a family, that there is evidence that their original problem is still causing them pain and that we are working only on those problems for which they requested and agreed on help.

By and large, we would always attempt direct, straight interventions in family problems first. If, after suggesting a number of perhaps exploratory tasks, it becomes obvious that the family is highly resistant (the family regularly "forgets" the task set, or makes sure it doesn't work, for instance) then we would begin to think about more paradoxical interventions. Moving from straight to paradoxical tasks may involve a fairly radical "change of tack" with a family but this can always be introduced to a family with comments like, "I/we didn't realise just how complex/serious/difficult this situation was . . .", or "I/we really hadn't appreciated how important so and so's behaviour was in this family . . .", or "we realise now that we've been barking up quite the wrong tree"!

It is frequently necessary to keep repeating a message to a family— therefore one needs to practise saying the same things in a dozen different ways. It is quite likely that one will need to keep going over the same ground during work with a family before "the penny drops" with the family, as it were. Messages sometimes take a while to sink in and so there may be a considerable gap between the first passing of a suggestion or comment on the system and any evidence that change in line with that suggestion or comment is occurring.

Minuchin (1974)[6] says people move (relationship-wise) for three reasons:
(a) they are challenged in their perceptions of reality,
(b) they are given alternative transactional patterns to work through,
(c) once they try out these new (more satisfactory) patterns of inter-action, this becomes self-reinforcing.

Changing beliefs through reframing is an effective way to achieve (a), especially if "straight" persuasion fails. When we set up a new game (by re-shaping family rules) we are achieving (b), but as regards (c) we make sure we take no credit and give that credit to the family itself.

E. *Co-therapy* Because of the resistance and the confusion of contradictory messages one encounters (the "icy blast" of disqualifications) support and morale boosting are necessary. We find these in the co-therapy partnership. A most supportive aspect of this partnership is that it encourages planning. Our plans for our sessions, more than anything else, help us to avoid getting bogged down. Agreement over who is responsible at each point of the session means that one worker can be thinking "has my partner covered his/her point sufficiently and should I come in now with my next point?" This gives momentum. We do not linger on a point more than is necessary (though we may repeat it within the same and in later sessions) and we can cover a great deal of ground in an hour. Of course one cannot plan for every contingency and one has to allow for the unexpected. It would be quite inappropriate to plough on with a plan regardless. We rather use the plan as a guide and backcloth. It is like having the tune (or beat) in one's head while dancing in step with the system. One responds to the family's concerns and inputs but keeps the plan in mind. We find that planning helps us to achieve more of the aims of our work with a family—we are less likely to get side-tracked down blind alleys, for instance, and more likely to achieve positive changes in as brief a time as possible. Co-therapy makes it easier to get started too and so if the reader is hesitating about starting we would urge him or her to find another interested worker, not necessarily from one's own agency. Get a sheet of paper, sort out one's understanding of the family's problems and hence one's goals and then focus on the aims for the first meeting. Draw up a plan together. Nothing works in some cases but one may well succeed with families where one would normally fail.

Whether one works on one's own or with a co-worker the reader will find that attaching himself or herself to a consultative/support/interest group is enormously valuable. We are linked to one which meets every month. We discuss each other's work, using brainstorming techniques to work out problems, goals and tasks and we monitor progress in work with families from month to month. Members of the group have teamed up with each other on some cases or have continued to work on their own with others. If there is no group already in existence in the reader's area, why not establish one? There are probably more people trying out family therapy ideas in one's area than one may imagine, especially if one approaches workers in other statutory or voluntary social work agencies.

The above five aspects make up the key features of our approach. We find that the method is economical to use. Six sessions or so with a family, with gaps of about 3 or 4 weeks between sessions (to allow time for the family to do its "homework" and absorb the content of the previous session), are often enough to produce limited, but "good enough" change which the family is happy to settle with. Carrying on beyond this stage of "minimum sufficient change" is, in our opinion, often counterproductive. In other words, terminate work whilst everyone feels that some success has been achieved. New contracts for further work can always be negotiated at a later date if the family requests additional help. The case of the Green family as presented in Part II of our book, showing full process recordings of the sessions, may give the reader the impression that an enormous amount of work is involved. However, as we mentioned in the Introduction we do not wish to suggest that family therapy work needs to be recorded so fully. We do believe though that each session needs to be planned in detail and thoroughly evaluated afterwards, whether one is working alone or with a co-therapist.

Adopting a family therapy approach in some cases makes a pleasant change from the routine work in which many workers are often involved. It is a stimulating method of work which will probably inspire readers in the other aspects of their practice. And, of course, it is the method of choice in a number of situations. Consider, for example, those cases where a young person is the client (perhaps subject to a Supervision Order). Referring to our selection charts in Chapter 2 one should consider firstly whether a family assessment is indicated and secondly whether a family therapy approach is likely to be most effective, bearing in mind that this can mean work with a part of the family, e.g. the parents, as much as with the whole family.

It is our hope that this small book will have given the reader a theoretical base and a practical method for his or her work. We find this approach works and we believe it could work for others too. If, however, readers find that other ideas and strategies feel comfortable for them and are effective please let us know. Similarly if our suggestions are helpful or otherwise do write to us (c/o Huddersfield Polytechnic).

References

1. Palazzoli, M. S., Boscolo, L., Cecchin, G. and Prata, G. *Paradox and counterparadox: A new model in the therapy of the family in schizophrenic transaction*, Jason Aronson Ltd., London (1978).
2. The First Annual International Conference of the Women's Project in *Family Therapy*, The dilemma of women in families. Held at Central Hall, London S.W.1 on June 26th and 27th, 1981.
3. Cade, B. Strategic Therapy, in *Journal of Family Therapy* **2**, 89–99 (1980)
4. The First Annual International Conference of the Women's Project in *Family Therapy, Op. Cit.*
5. Mueller, P. S. *et al. Op. Cit.* (Chapter 4) (1976)
6. Minuchin, S. *Families and Family Therapy*, Tavistock Pubs (1974).

Appendix A—Facilitative Exercises and Tasks

In this appendix we are bringing together a number of suggestions for tasks and exercises which may come in useful when working with families, either within sessions or as family "homework". They come from a number of sources and we have included a full reference list at the end.

The appendix is in two parts. Part A offers 18 suggestions for tasks that further the work of assessment. We suggest that probably only about three of these will need to be used with any one family. (We often use question-naires, like the one shown on pages 59–60, diagrammatic sculpts as described in Chapter 7 and Wants charts—No. 18 in the Appendix.) Then one should have enough information (after two or three exploratory sessions) to introduce interventive tasks, although, as we have commented in Chapter 2, there is never a clear-cut separation between assessment and treatment in practice. Part B lists several examples of interventive tasks that help people work towards their objectives. We have grouped these on a table to match the objectives for which they are designed. We hope that readers will carefully seek to select tasks that relate to the needs of a case and adjust tasks to meet the characteristics and requirements of each client system. Interven-tive tasks are NOT to be used at random or on a whim. Tasks should only be used when there is a problem that the family wishes to overcome. The sequences maintaining the problem should then be thoroughly analysed before designing an appropriate task tailored to achieving what the family wants and no more. These are obviously only a small selection of the exercises and tasks that have ever been described but generally they have wide applicability and are easily implemented. No doubt the reader will also want to design his or her own tasks and exercises to suit particular families with their special brand of problem/s.

A. Assessing Families and their Problems

Two writers (Ogden and Zevlin) describe three exercises in their book on assessing families which seem interesting:

1. Draw a house

Get the whole family to draw a house together without talking to each other; then get them all to indicate in the house, or on the paper, their own individual spaces.

The point of this exercise is to see how the family communicates, negotiates and generally interacts together during an active period without any talking among members. And one obtains their image of their living space and an idea of how each individual sees h/herself in relationship to the living space. Therefore one watches the process of their drawing the house as well as analysing the end-product.

Need a large piece of paper (3′ × 6′), a box of large crayons and enough floor space so people can move around freely.

Directions to the family—"This is a nonverbal exercise—that means no talking to each other or to me. I'd like you to use these crayons and this paper to draw a house together for your family. You have ten minutes". (Don't let them discuss what sort of house they'll draw—real, ideal etc.)

(Don't respond to complaints or jokes about not being able to talk.)

(Remind them about putting themselves in the drawing after 7 minutes.)

After the drawing time ask each family member "What house were you drawing?", and ask the whole family "Were there surprises or were all of you aware what house you were drawing together?" (Allow 30 minutes in all.)

2. Role card game

Have family members, without talking, pick out cards (listed below but other interaction roles and jobs could be included) for themselves and each other. The cards describe household job roles during dinner-evening-bed-time and certain kinds of interaction roles. Each member has a chance to state agreement or disagreement about the accuracy of each card for each person in the family and a chance at the end to reject the cards he/she does not want to keep.

Job roles (24)

Household organiser	Drink master	Gives small kids baths
Food shopper	Cook	Puts kids to bed
Meal planner	Table setter	Outdoor worker
Floor washer	Table cleaner	Holiday manager
Big filthy jobs	Washes dishes	Rule maker
Errand runner	Dries dishes	Disciplinarian
Fixer	After meal kitchen clean up	Responsible for everything
Cleans up after snacks	Pet feeder	Trash person

Interaction roles (12)

Positive	Negative
Truthteller	Blamer
Helpful one	Placator
Understanding one	Computer
Creative one	Lone wolf
Happy person	Distractor
Negotiator	Victim

The point of this exercise is to find out, in a non-threatening way, how the members see themselves and each other in terms of job and interaction roles. You look for discrepancies between how a member sees h/self and how others see him/her. You will see how household jobs are distributed and whether all members are satisfied with that distribution. Also, you will observe the family interacting in a nonverbal situation with a great deal of structure.

Need 36 (or more) role cards; a piece of paper, a pencil and a rubber band for each family member and a table around which everyone can comfortably sit (or use the floor).

Seat the family round the table and give each member a piece of paper with his or her name on it and a pencil. Spread all the cards out face up so everyone can see them and ask each of them to pick up those cards that are accurate for him or her. Each family member should place these cards in front of them for all to see. (If someone has picked a card another person would have done, that person should note it on his or her piece of paper.) ALL THIS HAS TO BE DONE WITHOUT TALKING.

Get each person to check out if he or she is satisfied with the cards before him or her.

Then ask each person to study everyone else's cards and note on their own piece of paper where they disagree with someone else's assessment of their jobs or interaction roles, e.g. "I don't think Mum is an errand runner", "I think Dad is a disciplinarian as well as Mum".

As a result of the above instruction people should next note if they think a job or role ascribed to them by someone else is wrong.

Next people can note which cards they would like to get rid of—jobs or roles they dislike. Put these on a separate pile.

Then spend some time discussing the cards and notes on paper which people are left with.

(This is simplifying Ogden's and Zevlin's game somewhat. They point out that one could use the cards to go on to negotiate a redistribution of jobs and roles. Actually swapping cards seems to have more of an impact.)

(Small children may need to be helped with this exercise.)

3. Family Bonanza

Tell the family they've won £100,000 on the pools. Ask the members to write down how each would like the family to spend the money; then ask members to negotiate together how the family will spend the money, each trying to get what he/she wants.

The point of this exercise is to see how the family negotiates when presented with money and the prospect of pleasure. Can members communicate directly with one another? Can they get what they want individually and as a family? Are they imaginative and open to change? Do parents model good negotiating for the children? Is the family able to make a decision?

Look at the process of discussion *and* at what they decide to buy with the money.

4. Family Life Space Drawings

As well as family sculpts telling one a lot about how people are with each other in families, drawings can also tell one a great deal. In session 2 of our case presentation (Chapter 7) we describe the drawings the Green family did for us. We have come across an article by Geddes and Medway and they suggest some refinements. Their article is worth reading in full but, summarising their ideas considerably, they suggest drawing a large circle on a blackboard or easel (we've used plain paper without problems). They then state that "The family is told that everything inside this family circle represents what they feel is part of their family. Persons and institutions felt not to be part of their family are placed outside of the family circle in the environment. The family circle and the environment represent the family life space". Then the family members are invited to, in turn, place themselves in the family circle using a small circle to represent themselves. Geddes and Medway recommend that the identified patient should not be invited to place themselves first—perhaps the most co-operative family member should be first invited. Immediate feedback is given to the family member with remarks like "so you feel you are very close to . . . far from . . . in the centre of the family etc. etc." The family is then invited to place any other significant people in its life in or around the circle (e.g. absent family members, friends, dead or living) and finally the family is invited to locate important social institutions (e.g. school, work, church, social agencies) in the environment. Where family members disagree about people's positions these are noted on the diagram. The next stage involves asking family members to indicate how they feel they communicate with the people and institutions located in the family's life space. Good communication is indicated by a solid straight line, so-so communication by a dotted line and poor communication by a slashed solid, straight line. Again feedback is given as people note the quality of their communication channels, e.g. "So you feel you can't talk to your mother, you have good communication with your father" etc.

Example of a family life space (fictitious family)

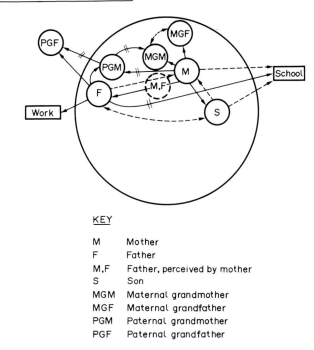

KEY

M	Mother
F	Father
M,F	Father, perceived by mother
S	Son
MGM	Maternal grandmother
MGF	Maternal grandfather
PGM	Paternal grandmother
PGF	Paternal grandfather

Information gleaned includes: A muddled family structure with grandparents getting in the way of Father's and Mother's relationships. Mother and Father disagree about how they communicate with each other, so do Mother and Son. There is poor communication between the two grandmothers and both grandmothers are said to have so-so or poor communications with their husbands. Mother thinks Father is closer to her than he thinks he is.

Geddes and Medway suggest that the three purposes of the family life space symbolic drawing are: (a) it provides a diagnostic source providing information about the family's structure, (b) family congruence can be gauged—do people agree on *where* people are in the family and outside of it and on how they communicate with each other, (c) it helps to identify the baseline from which change can be monitored.

(Obviously therapists can work out their own specialities of such drawings, to suit their own style of work.)

5. *Family Portraits*

(To help family members develop a broader, more objective view of their family.)

(a) Imagine that a stranger is coming to visit you. He has never met your family and someone is to meet him at the train.

How would each member of your family describe the others?

(Discuss immediately or write down each member's perceptions of the others first.)

Or

(b) Imagine that someone is writing a biography of each member of your family. What would each member say about the others in response to interview questions like:

What are his likes and dislikes?

What does he care about most?

What kind of things turn him off?

What kind of person is he?

Also describe yourself.

Or

(c) Use one adjective to describe each member of the family.

Or

(d) Sculpt how you feel each member is—arrange his body in a position that seems to you to characterise something about him.

Or

(e) Get one or more family members to sculpt the family group in order to get an idea of the emotional relationships between family members—the alliances, distances etc.

(Family members could, instead of actually producing a "physical tableau" with the group, put their ideas on paper, in diagrammatic form.)

(Lewis and Streitfeld.)

6. *Family History/process of becoming*

(i) Family trees/genograms:

Get the family to describe its origins—details of maternal and paternal grandparents, when and how husband and wife met etc. This kind of information can be represented diagrammatically, on paper or blackboard.

Uses of such material:

(i) may provide important diagnostic clues;

(ii) may help to reduce unhelpful tension;

(iii) often interests children and hence facilitates their involvement;

(iv) may increase family members' empathy.

(Walrond-Skinner.)

(ii)   Lifelines—"snakes".

Lifelines can be completed by individual family members about themselves (and then shared) or the family could work on identifying the family's own lifeline, together or separately.

e.g. imagine that the line drawn on this sheet of paper represents the course of your family's life. Starting from when Mr. and Mrs.——
——— married, and moving down the line, note down the significant events in the family's life. Note down the approximate dates and the effect of the event on family members (feelings and practical effects.)

Date	Event
1956	Mr. and Mrs.———— got married (or Mum and Dad married), Mum's family didn't approve.
1957	Billy was born—not an easy birth, relieved he was O.K.
1957	Dad had an accident at work-off for a long time, finances tight.
	etc.
	etc.
	etc.

(Adapted from Priestley *et al.*)

The following exercises are aimed specifically at helping a family to identify its problems:

7. Sentence completion exercise

"Our biggest problem is . . ."

"We also have problems with . . ."

Get family members to complete sentences like these, either as a group or as individuals, writing them down or telling each other—should provoke further discussion.

8. Problem check lists

(Again to generate further discussion.)

e.g.	Often a problem	Sometimes a problem	Never a problem
We row about little things			
People don't say what they mean			

	Often a problem	Sometimes a problem	Never a problem
We never do things together as a family			
The children never do as they are told			
We don't talk about things that matter			
Some people don't pull their weight in this family			

The family (as a group or as individuals) could be asked to indicate with a tick whether a particular statement applies to their family, and if so, with what degree of frequency.

(Workers can compile their own lists of statements—the above are only suggestions.)

9. Brainstorming Exercises

This is a widely-used method for helping groups to produce large quantities of ideas. It fits into any stage of the problem-solving process but it is particularly useful during assessment for creating lists of concerns and for exploring the feelings surrounding them.

All that is needed for brainstorming is a blackboard or a large sheet of paper on a wall, and something to write with.

Explain to the family that the aim of a brainstorming session is to generate as many ideas as possible on a given topic. The basic rules of the exercise are:

(a) Suspend judgement—the value of the ideas can be sorted out later.
(b) Aim for quantity not quality.
(c) Let the mind wander—wild and quirky ideas can turn out to be winners.
(d) Build on ideas of others—respond to what is already written up, add to it, expand it.

The title of the topic or problem is written at the top of the sheet and family members call out the ideas that occur to them and these are written up as quickly as possible, which usually means as one-word abbreviations.

(examples of topics = Family problems—we have problems with . . .

Family strengths—what we like about our family.

Family grievances—what we don't like about each other.)

The generation of such quantities of ideas (which may later be sorted out into smaller lists of related ideas) provide an initial snapshot of a family's concerns and can be used as a basis for further discussion.

(Adapted from Priestley *et al.*)

10. Air your grievances

Children and parents often surprise each other with their revelations.

(Lewis and Streitfeld.)

The following exercises are useful in trying to analyse problems:

11. The "5 W—H" System

Ask in relation to any problem, the questions:

What (is the problem?)
Who (does it affect?)
Where (does it happen?)
When (does it happen?)
Why (does it happen?)

and

How (could it be tackled?)

(Priestley *et al.*)

12. Force field analysis

This is essentially an application of brainstorming methods to the business of analysing problems. One generates lists of those forces which keep a problematic situation in being and those which push for its extinction/resolution. Once these "restraining" forces and "driving" forces have been identified decisions can be made about how to tackle the problem. Often working on the restraining forces is most productive.

e.g. Habit
      Friends do it/social poise, image   = RESTRAINING FORCES
      If not smoke = more food   (to induce smoking)
      Reduces tension
      Enjoy taste
      Relieves boredom
      Advertising pressure

PROBLEM = SMOKING

      After taste
      Health—cancer
      Short of breath
      Money—cost   = DRIVING FORCES
      Discolours teeth   (to reduce smoking)
      House and clothes smell
      Habit—no self control

Undertaking a force field analysis of a problem makes one:

(a) aware of the many forces maintaining a problem,
(b) look beyond the obvious and into new responses to the problem condition, and
(c) focus on the possible repercussions of any decisions.

' (Napier and Gershenfeld.)

13. Family Argument

Simulate a family argument (perhaps using video equipment for playback purposes)—e.g. what to watch on TV , what to do at the weekend or an argument that is constantly repeated in the family's day-to-day life.

Either

Sit in a circle and speak in order. Each person may say only one sentence when his turn comes. Continue until there is some sort of resolution and then discuss what happened.

Or

Allow the family to argue "naturally".

Questions that might be asked:

What do you perceive about yourself and the others as the argument progresses?

How do you feel when you are talking?

How do you feel when the other family members talk?

Do roles or patterns emerge?

   e.g. Placators, attackers, evaders.

Does one person always dominate? Submit?

Who makes whom feel threatened? Angry, ashamed, resentful?

Do people say what they mean?

(Lewis and Streitfeld.)

The following exercises help families to work out their objectives:

14. Ranking

The family, as individuals and as a group, can be asked to rank the problems they have identified in order of:

   urgency,
   importance,
   or difficulty.

15. Sentence Completion

"What I (we) most want to do about (this problem) is . . ."

"Next time this (situation) happens I (we) will . . ."

"To do (such and such) I (we) will first of all need to . . ."

Families can complete these or similar sentences one or more times as the situation requires.

or

Families could be asked to complete the sort of table outlined below:

Problem	Steps towards solving this problem could be . . .
Our biggest problem is	
We also have problems with	
We also have problems with	

16. Brainstorming

Brainstorming can be used to help generate objectives.

17. Ideal Family

(a) Compose imaginary classified advertisements headed: "Father wanted" etc. in 20/30 words.

(b) Compose similar adverts. headed: "Son (mother, father, etc.) available" in which one lists one's own attributes.

18. Asking for what you want

Get each member to write on a card what they want most from each other member of the family and what they think each other member wants from them.

Then get each member to directly ask all the other members for what they want most from them, without referring to the cards.

After that get each member to write on another card what each person asked them for, whether or not they think they can give it to that person and whether or not they think they can get what they asked for from that person.

The point of this exercise is to see if the individuals in the family can be honest about their wants and needs, can communicate them directly to each other and can have them heard and understood.

Cards can be laid out like the ones below:

WANT CARD Side 1

JOHN	
I want from Mary:	
I want from Billy:	
I want from Ann:	

WANT CARD Side 2

JOHN	
Mary wants from me:	
Billy wants from me:	
Ann wants from me:	

QUESTION CARD

John	What did each person ask you for?	Do you think you can give it to them?	Do you think you can get what you asked them for?
MARY			
BILLY			
ANN			

(Ogden and Zevin.)

We have adapted these suggestions to design our own "WANTS SHEET" and we ask members of a family to complete a sheet each. Frequently people are pleasantly surprised by each others' replies! These sheets are typed on a page of A4 paper, as in the following example:

Completed by: Betty Names	What I want from them.	My chance of getting it.	What they want from me.	What chance that I can give it to them?
Dad				
Mum				
Liz				
Jimmy				

B. Working towards objectives

In other parts of the book we discuss ways of working towards objectives through various means and tasks may flow naturally from the previous "assessment oriented" exercises. Below we list some other ideas for possible tasks and at the end we offer some guidance about when tasks may be appropriately used.

19. Exercises involving role play

(i)   "Turnabout" or Role reversal:

Get family members to switch roles, e.g. when confronted by a sub-grouping such as mother and son or husband and wife who are locked in conflict. The therapist would suggest that the pair exchange roles and play each other's parts. Used in this way, role reversal can be a powerful technique for increasing mutual empathy and bringing about conflict resolution.

(ii)   Action replays:

Get family members to role play typical family arguments instead of just endlessly discussing them—these may be recorded with video or audio tape equipment, or the worker(s) can provide feedback, make suggestions for future ways of dealing with the situation etc. (which could then be rehearsed).

(iii)   Play back by workers:

After observing a piece of interaction between family members (e.g. the marital couple) workers with the family can decide to play back the action, by becoming the alter-egos of the family members involved (expressing both verbal and non-verbal aspects of the interaction). Sentences beginning "I never realised before that I . . ." are a common response from the family members.

(Walrond-Skinner.)

20. Physical Re-arrangements

Geographic re-arrangement of seating positions can be used as a means of interpreting and changing a family's structure, e.g. to reinforce the husband-wife pairing, to modify the relationship between a father and his children.

(Walrond-Skinner.)

21. Exercises to improve communication channels in a family

(i)   Condensed conversations:

Sit facing your partner and have a conversation using a single word at a time (or a sentence)—which expresses how you are feeling towards your partner at that moment.

Sometimes it may be useful to cut out all non-verbal communication by placing family members with their backs to each other—e.g. so children, for instance, aren't prevented from speaking by their parents' non-verbal cues.

(Walrond-Skinner.)

(ii) Opening New Lines:
Virginia Satir suggests this for some couples:
1. First stand back-to-back and talk to each other (like in the kitchen perhaps).
2. Then stand face-to-face and look at each other without talking. What do you think your partner is thinking and feeling? In discussion, note how wrong your assumptions may have been.
3. Now eyeball each other and communicate only with gestures and touches. See how much more gets through?
4. Close your eyes and communicate without talking.
5. Eyeball each other and talk without touching.
6. Finally use all forms of communication—talk, touch and look at each other.

(iii) What do you mean?
As message giver, consciously make an effort to say what you mean (perhaps by using only "I . . ." statements). As receiver tell your partner when you think you're getting a garbled signal. Some therapists have couples carry on a conversation asking each other after every statement "What do you mean?"

(iv) Intimate talk:
Get people to initiate a conversation about something they've never talked about before, or at least not in a great while.

(v) The cushion exercise:
The cushion exercise involves one member holding a cushion, or any light object. Only that member may speak, the others have to give a hand signal when they wish to have the object passed to them so that they may speak. This is an excellent exercise for calming a session with a noisy family, where people do not listen to each other and hence have to shout to try and get themselves heard.
A variation on the "cushion exercise". A "speaker's chair" may be designated and only the person sitting in that chair is allowed to talk.

(vi) Father and mother may be directed to talk without including daughter within an interview session, or mother and son may be told to talk without father interrupting.

22. *Various tasks (some straight, some more paradoxical)*

(i) Parents may be asked to "watch carefully for positive behaviour" in their child's problematic behaviour—they may be asked to keep notes/records of such positive behaviour. This would probably be said in the context of reframing the child's behaviour as normal, given the child's age, stage of development and hence likely to improve only gradually as a result of maturation. Such a task may help in instances where people have got stuck in a rut of only noticing the worst aspects of their child's functioning.

To be specific, a child could be asked, in the parents' hearing, to be their usual self but to try to elude the parents in such a way that it will be harder for them to get a full list of good behaviours, i.e. the child or teenager tries to see how many helpful.bits of behaviour they can perform without being noticed. (This changes the old game of criticism and sets up a new game—catching the child being good.)

(ii) "An individual or family may be told that during the coming week they will spontaneously get an idea that will improve their situation. They may be told they are at a stage where they are responsive now to ideas from within themselves. This task helps patients initiate change".

(Haley.)

(iii) "In two or three generational conflicts, get the parties to do things which will 'force' more appropriate realignments.

e.g. where grandmother is siding with granddaughter against the mother, see the mother and grandchild together. The child should be instructed to do something of a minor nature that would irritate the grandmother and the mother is asked to defend her daughter against the grandmother.

e.g. where one parent is inappropriately siding with one child against the other parent, devise a task, suited to their situation, which forces the parents together and breaks up the problematic coalition".

(Haley.)

e.g. where a father is over-involved in seeking to control a teenage daughter and a mother is under-involved, ask mother and daughter to spend some time together (uninterrupted by the others in the family) and to keep the content of that "Special Time" SECRET. (Secrets forge alliances.) They could also be asked to spend some of that time planning a surprise for Dad, or (if one thinks Dad could stand it) planning for the daughter to annoy her father in some small way—in which case mother would promise to support her against father. (This latter suggestion would have to be given without father's knowledge.)

e.g. where a mother and child are over involved with each other, father and mother could be asked to have a discussion about involving another, rather neglected child or they could be asked to find ways of involving the father with the first child more, e.g. helping the child with homework, sharing a joint interest or hobby.

e.g. if a father is regularly too intrusive in the handling of a child, he and his wife could be asked to devise a system whereby she helps him to control his involvement, e.g. she might squeeze his arm as a secret signal to pull back from over-involvement.

(iv) In disorganised families tasks could be set which demand that they list activities planned for the week in order to bring some order into things. If household chores are a bone of contention, lists could be drawn up of the chores needing to be done and by whom. A "monitor" might be appointed (usually a parent, sometimes a child) to supervise this and record peoples' performances.

(v) In families where people are always trying to disqualify each other, a task could be set which keeps bringing this insidious practice into peoples' consciousness. When anyone feels disqualified they are to say to the disqualifier calmly and matter-of-factly, "You are disqualifying me and I do not accept that". This has the effect of disrupting habitual, unproductive interaction.

(vi) The last sort of task (v) could be linked to tasks which encourage people to give each other "positive strokes", i.e. positive comments, non-verbal expressions of warmth and affection, e.g. gifts or actions which appreciate someone and signify the worth and esteem in which they are held, and so on. Lists could be kept of positive strokes *given* and *received* (giving lifts one's own self esteem) in any one day and comparisons made with previous days' lists. Targets for increased positive stroking could be negotiated!

People may not know what pleases others—couples may have been playing "cat and mouse" with each other for years. In this case a rule could be established that the recipient of a "positive stroke" should always say "thank you" to the giver and indicate what it was that gave them pleasure.

(vii) Ask people to make efforts to show interest in each other, e.g. get family members to ask each other two personal questions each day.

(viii) Get people to *reverse* the way they normally behave towards each other. For example, if a wife is feeling controlled by her husband's intrusive, dominating, over-protective behaviour, take him on one side and suggest he eases off in various ways, by way of experimentation, to try out a new role or even for a bit of fun and/or mischief. It is important that the wife is surprised by her husband's change in his behaviour towards her, if maximum therapeutic benefit is to be achieved.

(Peggy Papp suggests as we've indicated earlier in the book, that in these sorts of situations the husband's over-controlling behaviour can be positively reframed as "being like a mother" and the wife's depression or acting out behaviour as "adolescent rebellion". The husband can then be encouraged to let his wife "grow up" by giving her more independence and self-responsibility and the wife can be helped to "grow up" and show that she is capable of more mature functioning.)

(ix) "In another case, a husband is asked to do something for his wife that she would not expect and she is asked to receive it graciously. He cannot do something routine, which she would expect, and therefore he is encouraged to initiate something new in the marriage. He also must think about his wife carefully to decide on something she would not expect".

(Haley.)

A useful task where marriages have become rather "stale".

A variation on this involves asking, for instance, the wife (on her own) to relate to her husband in ways that she knows will give him pleasure but without "publicising" her behaviour. He would be given the task of spotting and noting down these "pleasures".

(x) "A mother and father who need an excuse to be affectionate with each other may be asked to show affection to each other in an obvious way at set times to "teach their child" how to show affection".

(Haley.)

(xi) Get people in conflict to list what they like about each other and what makes them annoyed. Get them to list detailed items of behaviour, e.g. "I can't stand the way he doesn't put the top on the toothpaste tube", "She is a terribly bossy back-seat driver", "I love the way he strokes my hair gently while we are watching TV together", "I think the way she cooks curries is great". People should then be brought together to compare and discuss their lists.

Tasks could be worked out that link the items that give people pleasure, which they've included in their lists. For instance, if a husband likes real ale, if the wife likes a break from cooking and the kids like trips out, the scene is set for a splendid family outing!

(xii) Relegate negative aspects of interaction to certain times of the day or week. For instance, designate a time of day, when everyone is around, as the family's argument period. Potential arguments brewing up outside of the argument period have to be saved up until then. The task may be suggested in the context of a comment that families need to be able to argue, that arguing is an important aspect of family life.

Families could also be asked to practise ending arguments in constructive, amicable ways, or to practise dealing pleasantly with a particularly provocative family member.

(xiii) If people regularly get "worked up" by things around them offer suggestions about how they might relax.

e.g. through taking regular physical exercise—swimming is an excellent activity. (Don't forget positive *physical* strokes—massaging backs, feet, necks.)

e.g. through learning how to control stress. We have become

interested in the possibility of using the commercially sold small versions of bio-feedback machines. They help people to become aware of when they are tense and over time they can learn to regulate their stress levels. Such machines have, apparently, been used successfully in the treatment of high blood pressure.

e.g. Whirlpool exercise—when hot and bothered, imagine you are in a pool of muddy, sandy water that is swirling about, all dark. Concentrate on imagining you are slowing down the water so the muddiness can settle. It slows down as your mind becomes calm and the water clears and the sun shines through as you rest (like a mermaid!) on the still, calm sandy bottom, full of peace etc. (*NB* Other aspects of yoga and meditation may help.)

In addition to the above tasks it may be more appropriate to devise other tasks to suit a particular family's problems and circumstances. When doing this Haley suggests that the steps in designing a task are to think about the presenting problem in terms of the sequence in the family and to find a directive that changes both. This obviously requires practice and experience. Involving other people in task design, perhaps brainstorming possibilities may help too. However, in relation to the tasks 19–22 above we offer below a table which attempts to suggest the most appropriate tasks for the kinds of family difficulties described in earlier chapters which seem responsive to a family therapy approach.

ASSESSMENT	OUR PREFERRED TASKS	OTHER POSSIBILITIES
Problems arising out of mishandling ordinary difficulties.	22i); 22xii); 22xiii), 22viii)	19; 22ii);
System boundary problems, arising out of lack of clear boundaries	20; In addition meet with the various sub-systems separately.	4.
Inappropriate alliances that need to be changed	22iii);	4; In general tasks that unite parents will reduce inappropriate parent-child alliances.
Family enmeshment, general role confusion	22iv);	2; 22iii); In addition meet with sub-systems separately; Also agree privacy/personal space rules.
Communication problems.	21v);	1; 3; 18; 21; 22xi); 19.
Relationship problems generally.	22v); 22vi); 22vii); 22ix);	5; 22viii); 22x);

Source Material

(1) Sue Walrond-Skinner, *Family therapy: the treatment of natural systems*, Lib. S/W, R.K.P. (1976.)

(2) Gina Ogden and Anne Zevin, *When a family needs therapy*, Beacon Press. (1976.)

(3) Peggy Papp (Ed.), *Family therapy: Full length case studies*, Gardner Press Inc. (1977.)

(4) Philip Priestley, James McGuire, David Flegg, Valerie Hemsley and David Welham, *Social skills and personal problem solving*, Tavistock Publications. (1978.)

(5) H. R. Lewis and H. S. Streitfeld, *Growth Games*, Harcourt, Brace and Jovanovich Inc. (1970.)

(6) Jay Haley, *Problem solving therapy*, Jossey-Bass. (1976.)

(7) Michael Geddes and Joan Medway, The Symbolic Drawing of the Family Life Space, in *Family Process*, **16**, No. 2, pages 219–227. (1977.)

(8) R. W. Napier and M. K. Gershenfeld, *Groups: Theory and Experience*, Houghton Mifflin Co. (1973.)

(9) S. Minuchin and H. C. Fishman, *Family Therapy Techniques*, Harvard University Press, Cambridge, Mass. (1981.)

Index